Eugen Richter

Pictures of the socialistic future

Eugen Richter

Pictures of the socialistic future

ISBN/EAN: 9783337278175

Printed in Europe, USA, Canada, Australia, Japan

Cover: Foto ©Suzi / pixelio.de

More available books at **www.hansebooks.com**

PICTURES OF THE
SOCIALISTIC FUTURE

(Freely adapted from Bebel)

BY

EUGENE RICHTER

MEMBER OF THE IMPERIAL GERMAN PARLIAMENT

AUTHORISED TRANSLATION BY HENRY WRIGHT

LONDON
SWAN SONNENSCHEIN
PATERNOSTER SQUARE
1893

CONTENTS

		PAGE
I.	CELEBRATION-DAY	1
II.	THE NEW LAWS	4
III.	DISCONTENTED PEOPLE	6
IV.	THE CHOICE OF TRADES	8
V.	A PARLIAMENTARY SITTING	11
VI.	ASSIGNMENT OF WORK	16
VII.	NEWS FROM THE PROVINCES	22
VIII.	THE LAST DAY TOGETHER	26
IX.	THE GREAT MIGRATION	30
X.	THE NEW CURRENCY	34
XI.	THE NEW DWELLINGS	37
XII.	THE NEW STATE COOKSHOPS	42
XIII.	A VEXING INCIDENT	47
XIV.	A MINISTERIAL CRISIS	49
XV.	EMIGRATION	51
XVI.	RETIREMENT OF THE CHANCELLOR	54
XVII.	IN AND ABOUT THE WORKSHOPS	56
XVIII.	FAMILY MATTERS	60
XIX.	RECREATIONS OF THE PEOPLE	64
XX.	DISAGREEABLE EXPERIENCES	68
XXI.	FLIGHT	72
XXII.	ANOTHER NEW CHANCELLOR	76
XXIII.	FOREIGN COMPLICATIONS	78
XXIV.	THE ELECTION STIR	82
XXV.	SAD NEWS	88
XXVI.	THE RESULT OF THE ELECTIONS	90
XXVII.	A LARGE DEFICIT	93
XXVIII.	DOMESTIC AFFAIRS	97
XXIX.	A STORMY PARLIAMENTARY SITTING	100
XXX.	THREATENED STRIKE	119
XXXI.	MENACING DIPLOMATIC NOTES	121
XXXII.	GREAT STRIKE AND SIMULTANEOUS OUTBREAK OF WAR	124
XXXIII.	THE COUNTER-REVOLUTION BEGINS	126
XXXIV.	DISHEARTENING NEWS	129
XXXV.	THE LAST CHAPTER	131

PICTURES OF THE SOCIALISTIC FUTURE.

CHAPTER I.

CELEBRATION DAY.

THE red flag of international Socialism waves from the palace and from all the public buildings of Berlin. If our immortal Bebel could but have lived to see this! He always used to tell the bourgeoisie that "the catastrophe was almost at their very doors." Friedrich Engels had fixed 1898 as the year of the ultimate triumph of socialistic ideas. Well, it did not come quite so soon, but it has not taken much longer.

This, however, is immaterial. The main thing is the fact that all our long years of toil and battling for the righteous cause of the people are now crowned with success. The old rotten regime, with its ascendency of capital, and its system of plundering the working classes, has crumbled to pieces. And for the benefit of my children, and children's children, I intend to set down, in a humble way, some little account of the beginning of this new reign of brotherhood and universal philanthropy. I, too, have not been altogether without some small share in this new birth of mankind. All, both in time and money, that I have been able for a generation past to snatch from the practice of my craft as an honest bookbinder, and all that my family could spare, I have devoted to the furtherance of our aims. I am also indebted to the literature of Socialism, and to my connection with political clubs, for my mental culture and my soundness on all socialistic points. My wife and children are in full accord with me. Our beloved Bebel's book on women has long been the highest gospel to my better half, Paula.

The birthday of the new socialistic order happened to be our silver wedding-day; and now, behold, to-day's celebration day has added fresh happiness to us as a family. My son, Franz, has become engaged to Agnes Müller. The two have long known each other, and the strong attachment is mutual. So in all the elevation of mind, inspired by this great day, we have knit up this new bond of affection. They are both somewhat young yet, but they are, nevertheless, both good hands at their trades. He is a compositor, she a milliner. So there is ground to hope it will turn out a good match. They intend to marry as soon as the new regulations in respect of work, arrangements of dwellings, and so on, shall have reached completion.

After dinner we all took a stroll *unter den Linden*. My stars! what a crowd there was! And what endless rejoicing! Not one single discordant tone to mar the harmony of the great celebration day. The police is disbanded, the people themselves maintaining order in the most exemplary manner.

In the palace gardens, in the square in front, and all around the palace, vast crowds were gathered, which showed unmistakable unanimity and steadfastness of aim. The new Government was assembled in the palace. Colleagues, chosen from amongst the foremost leaders of the Socialist party, have provisionally taken over the reins of Government. The Socialist members of the town council form, for the present, the corporation. Whenever, from time to time, one of our new rulers chanced to show himself at one of the windows, or on a balcony, the uncontrollable ecstasy of the people would break out afresh, showing itself in frantic waving of hats and handkerchiefs, and in singing the workmen's Marseillaise.

In the evening there was a grand illumination. The statues of the old kings and marshals, decorated with red flags, looked strange enough in the red glare of so much bengal fire. The days of these statues are, however, numbered, and they will shortly have to give place to statues of bygone heroes of Socialism. It has already been determined, I hear, to remove the statues of the two Humboldts from the front of the university, and to place there in their stead those of Marx and Ferdinand Lassalle. The statue of Frederic the Great, *unter den Linden*, is to be replaced by that of our immortal Liebknecht.

Upon our return home we kept up, in our cosy family circle, this double celebration till a late hour. My wife's father, who hitherto has not made much account of Socialism, was with us on the occasion, and was very sympathetic and cheery.

We are full of hope that we shall now soon vacate our humble dwelling, three storeys high, and exchange it for something better. Well, well, the old place, after all, has witnessed many a quiet joy of ours, no lack of trouble and sorrow, and plenty of honest endeavour as well.

CHAPTER II.

THE NEW LAWS.

One hears the most exquisite stories of the scramble there is on the part of the bourgeoisie to get across the frontier. But where are they to go to? Socialism is now dominant in all European countries, with the exception of England and Switzerland. The American steamers are unable to meet the demand there is on them. Those who can once reach the American shores are all right, as the revolution there was very soon quelled, and all hope of success cut off for a long time to come. Let all such plunderers clear out, say I. It is a good thing that, thanks to the suddenness with which the revolution came at last, they have not been able to take much with them. All State bonds, mortgages, shares, bills, and bank-notes have been declared void. These bourgeois gentry may as well at once begin papering the walls of their ship cabins with this trumpery. All landed and house property, means of communication, machinery, tools, stores, and such like, have been impounded for the benefit of the new socialistic State.

The *Onward*, which has hitherto been the leading organ of our party, now takes the place of the old *Imperial Advertiser*, and it is delivered at every house free of cost. All printing establishments having now become the property of the State, all the other papers have, as a matter of course, ceased to appear. In all other towns a local edition of the *Onward* is issued with a sheet of local matter for each separate place.

Provisionally, and until such time as a new Parliament shall have been elected, the conduct of affairs is in the hands of the socialistic members of the late Parliament, who, in the shape of a Committee of Government, have to decide on those numerous laws it will be necessary to enact in order to establish the new era.

The old party programme which was settled upon at the Erfurt Conference in 1891, has been promulgated as an outline of the fundamental rights of the people. This promulgation proclaims that all capital, property, mines and quarries, machinery, means of communication, and all possessions whatever, have henceforth become the sole property of the State, or as it is now better called, the Community. Another decree sets forth the universal obligation there is on all persons to work; and all such persons, whether male or female, from the age of 21 to 65 years, are to enjoy precisely the same rights. Those who are below 21 years of age will be educated at the expense of the State, whilst those who are above 65 will be maintained in a similar manner. All private enterprise and productivity have, of course, ceased. Pending, however, the new regulations as to supply, all persons are to retain their old posts, and to go on working for the State, as their master. Each person has to render an inventory of all such things as may have remained to him after the embargo just spoken of; things which some might be tempted to regard as private property, such as furniture, old clothes, bank-notes, and the like. In particular, coins of all kinds are to be delivered up. New money certificates are shortly to be issued.

The new Government, thanks to the smart Chancellor at its head, proceeds with no less energy than directness of purpose. Every precaution in the first place is to be taken against any possibility of capital ever regaining its old ascendency. The army is disbanded; no taxes will be collected, as the Government proposes to raise that which is required for public purposes out of the revenue yielded by State trade transactions. Doctors and lawyers are supported by the State, and they are required to render their services gratis whenever needed. The days of the revolution, and of the celebration of the same, have been declared holidays established by law.

It is quite evident that entirely new and glorious times are in store for us.

CHAPTER III.

DISCONTENTED PEOPLE.

AGNES, our prospective daughter-in-law, is quite inconsolable, and Franz is hardly less depressed. Agnes is in fear for her dowry. For a long time past she has been industriously saving up, and more especially so since her acquaintance with Franz. Her industry was such that she would scarce allow herself time for her meals, and the sums which her companions spent in finery, in pleasures, or in short excursions, she devoted to the increase of her little capital. By these means she had no less a sum than two thousand marks in the savings bank at the time of her becoming engaged. It was with no little pride and complacency that Franz told me all this on the evening of the engagement day. The young people began to devise schemes as to how they could lay out this large sum of money to the best advantage.

But now it seems that all her industry and economy are to prove quite futile. Rendered uneasy by all sorts of reports that reached her, Agnes determined to go to the bank and give notice of withdrawal. Arrived in the neighbourhood of the bank, she found the street filled with excited groups. Old men and women, and numerous girls who had been servants during the old order of things, complained piteously of being cheated, as they said, out of their hard-earned savings. The officials, it appears, had stated that along with all other values which, by the operation of the new decrees had been confiscated, the funds of the savings bank were also void.

The mere rumour of such a thing nearly made poor Agnes faint. Summoning courage, however, to enter the bank, she there soon received confirmation of this incredible news. Hastening to us, she heard it rumoured that deputations of bank creditors were on their way to the palace to seek an interview with the Chancellor. On hearing this I started off at once, and Franz went with me.

We found an immense crowd gathered in front of the palace. Across Lassalle Bridge (the old King William's Bridge), streams of people kept surging up towards the palace. It is clear this savings bank question is deeply stirring the public mind. All the entrances to the courts of the palace were securely fastened. The crowd in front made various efforts to obtain forcible entrance, but in vain. Suddenly several gun-barrels from inside bristled through loopholes in the doors, which loopholes I had somehow never noticed before.

Who can say what might have been the end of all this if, at this critical moment, the Chancellor had not appeared on the scene and thus restored order? He stepped out upon the balcony of the middle portal, and in a clear and sonorous voice, declared that the savings bank question should receive the immediate consideration of the Committee of Government. He begged all true patriots and consistent Socialists to confide fully in the justice and wisdom of the representatives of the people. Loud hurrahs greeted our Chancellor as he withdrew.

Just at this moment several fire brigades came tearing along at a gallop from different directions towards the palace. There being now no police to summon, the authorities had in their consternation telegraphed from the palace, reporting a great fire there. The arrival of the gallant fellows was greeted with much laughter. By and by the crowd dispersed in a more good-humoured and pliant mood. It is only to be hoped that the Government will do the right thing in this business.

CHAPTER IV.

THE CHOICE OF TRADES.

BIG red placards on all the hoardings remind people that in accordance with the regulations of the new Labour Law, all persons of both sexes, between the ages of twenty-one and sixty-five years, are required within three days to register themselves with a view to being told off to some trade. The old police stations and various other public offices come in nicely for this purpose. The attention of women and girls is especially called to the fact that on their entering upon work in one of the numerous State workshops, they are forthwith relieved from all household toil, such as taking care of children, the preparation of meals, nursing the sick, washing, etc., etc. All children and young people are to be brought up in State maintenance houses and in public schools. The chief meal of each day will be taken at the State cookshop of the district. Sick people must all be sent to the hospitals. Washing can be done solely at the great central washhouses of the State. The hours of work, for both sexes, both in trades and in State or public departments, are fixed at eight hours for the present.

Documentary evidence is in all cases required as a proof of the capabilities of persons to perform the duties they enter themselves for; and in each case the business hitherto followed has to be stated as well. Entries as clergymen cannot for a moment be entertained, seeing that by a resolution come to at the Erfurt Conference of 1891, and which is now accepted as a fundamental law of the State, it is strictly prohibited to devote any national funds to religious or ecclesiastical purposes. Such persons, however, who, nevertheless, wish to follow this profession, have full liberty to qualify themselves for it in their leisure hours, after having worked the normal number of eight hours in some branch which is recognised by the State as a trade.

After the publication of this intelligence, the life in the streets resembled that on a mustering day in a garrison town. Persons of the same trade formed themselves into knots and groups, and having decorated themselves with some sign of the trade chosen, marched through the streets singing and shouting. There were numerous groups of women and girls, who painted in the liveliest colours the delights they anticipate from the trades chosen, now that they have once got rid of all housework. One hears that a great many persons have chosen an entirely different line from the one hitherto followed. Many seem to fancy that the mere choice of a trade is identical with being already installed in it, but such is, of course, by no means the case.

So far as we as a family are concerned we mean to make no change, but to remain faithful to those old trades we have got to like; so my son Franz, my future daughter-in-law Agnes, and I myself have entered our names accordingly. My wife has registered herself as an attendant at one of the children's homes. By this means she proposes still to exercise her maternal care over our youngest child Annie, four years of age, whom we shall now, of course, have to yield up.

I may here mention that after the tumult in front of the palace, the Ministry deemed it prudent to reintroduce a body of police, which is to be four thousand strong, and to station them in part at the arsenal, and in part at the neighbouring barracks. With a view to avoiding all unpleasant reminiscences, the blue uniform will now be discontinued, and a brown one substituted for it. In place of a helmet the police are to wear large Rembrandt hats with red feathers.

CHAPTER V.

A PARLIAMENTARY SITTING.

It was only with considerable trouble that Franz and I managed to-day to squeeze ourselves into the House situated in Bebel Square (the King's Square of old days). A settlement was to be arrived at in respect of the savings bank funds. Franz informs me that amongst the 2,000,000 inhabitants of Berlin, there are no fewer than 500,000 depositors in the savings banks. No wonder, then, that the whole neighbourhood of the House, the entire expanse of Bebel Square, and the surrounding streets, were densely packed with persons mostly of the poorer clad sort, who awaited with breathless interest the decision of the House. The police, however, soon began to clear the streets.

As the general election has not yet taken place, and as all the seats of those members who were elected by the so-called better classes were declared vacant, we found, as a matter of course, no other members present save our old colleagues the proved pioneers of the new order.

At the request of the Chancellor, the head of the Statistical Department opened the debate in a speech dealing largely with statistics, and showing the real magnitude of the question in hand. He said there were eight million depositors in the savings banks, with an aggregate of more than 5,000 millions of marks. (Hear, hear, from the Left.) The yearly sum formerly paid in interest amounted to more than 150 millions of marks. Of the deposits, 2,800 million marks were invested in mortgages, 1,700 millions in bonds, about 400 millions in public institutions and corporations, and the balance of 100 millions were floating debt. All bonds had been repudiated by law. (Quite right, from the Left.) With the transfer of all landed property to the State, all mortgages were, as a matter of course, annulled. It was, hence, clear that there were no funds out of which the claims of the savings bank depositors could be satisfied.

At the close of this speech a member of the Right got up. "Millions of honest workmen and true Socialists," said he (uproar from the Left), "will feel bitterly disappointed when, in place of getting the full reward of labour as expected, they see themselves deprived of those savings they had by dint of arduous work been enabled to put by. By what means had those savings been effected? Only by means of continuous effort and exertion, of economy, and of abstention from certain things, such as tobacco and spirits, which many other workmen often indulged in. (Uproar from the Left.) Many a one had imagined that by putting by these savings he was laying up something for a rainy day, or providing for his old age. The placing of such persons on precisely the same footing with those who have not shown a morsel of thrift, will be felt by millions to be an injustice." (Applause from the Right, and loud cries of approval from the galleries.)

The President threatened to have the galleries cleared if such cries were repeated, and at this there were cries, "We are the nation."

The President: "The nation is in possession of a power of veto, but it possesses no right to take part in the debates in Parliament. Disturbers will be ejected." (General approbation from all sides.)

A member of the Left now followed: "A real Socialist of pure water never yet had bothered himself about saving anything," said he. (Contradictory signs from the Right.) "Nobody who had allowed himself to follow the doctrines of economy so much preached by the bourgeoisie had the least right to reckon on any consideration at the hands of the socialistic State. Let it not be forgotten, too, that some of these savings were in reality only stolen from the working-classes. (Dissatisfaction from the Right.) It should never be said that Socialism had hung up the big thieves, but let millions of little ones escape. Why, the various investments of this very savings bank capital had helped to foster the old system of robbing the people. (Loud applause from the Left.) None but a bourgeois can say a word against the confiscation of the savings bank funds."

The President here called the last speaker to order for the grave offence implied in designating a member of the socialistic Parliament by the term bourgeois.

Amidst breathless suspense the Chancellor rose to speak. "Up to a certain point justice compels me to say that both the honourable members who have just spoken are quite right in what they have advanced. A good deal might be said on the side of the morality of these savings, but equally much may be advanced as to the demoralising effects they have exercised in the form of accumulated capital. Let us, however, above all things, never suffer a longing look at the past to divert our gaze from the great times in which we live. (Hear, hear.) We must settle this question as Socialists who know what they are about, and without any admixture of sentiment. And in view of this I say that to hand over 5,000 million marks to a fractional eight millions of the population would be a building up of the new social equality on a foundation of inequality. (Applause.) This inequality would inevitably soon make itself felt throughout all the various branches of consumption, and thus upset all our carefully conceived plans for harmonising production and consumption. These fund-holders to-day ask for a return of their savings : with precisely the same right others might come to-morrow —those, for instance, who had sunk their savings in machinery and tools, in business stock, in houses or land—and demand that their capital be refunded. (Signs of approval.) How are we then to set bounds to a possible reaction against the social order of things now established ? Whatever pleasures those persons who had put by their little savings had promised themselves as the fruits of their thrift, and their abstinence, they would now reap a hundred times greater reward in the consciousness of knowing that all alike will now share those great benefits which we are about inaugurating. But if you take from us these five milliards, reducing by this amount the capital which ought to work solely in the interests of the public at large, then my colleagues in the ministry, and myself, will be no longer in a position to accept the responsibility of carrying out those socialistic measures which it was our aim to see accomplished." (Loud and long-continued applause.)

A great number of members had signified their intention of speaking. But the President said it was his duty to remind the House that, reckoning the time spent on committee meetings, and that which the law allowed to each member for reading and preparation, the maximum eight hours had, as a matter of fact, already been reached, and that under these circumstances the debate could not be continued before the next day. (Cries of "vote, vote.") A resolution to apply the closure was proposed and passed. Upon the vote being taken, the House, with only a few dissentients, passed to the order of the day, and the sitting was over.

There were loud cries of indignation from the gallery, and these spread to the street outside. The police, however, soon managed to clear the space about the House, and they arrested various noisy persons, amongst whom were a good many women. It is said that several members who had voted against the bank monies being refunded to the owners were shamefully insulted in the streets. The police are stated to have made merciless use of their new weapons, the so-called "killers," a weapon on the English pattern which has just been introduced.

Within our four walls we had an abundant display of resentment and ill-feeling. Agnes rejected all endeavours to tranquillise her, and it was in vain that my wife sought to comfort her with the thought of the opulent dowry which the Government meant all newly married couples to receive.

"I won't have anything given to me," she cried pettishly; "all I want is the wages of my own labour; such government is worse than robbery."

I much fear that to-day's events are not at all calculated to strengthen Agnes' hold on socialistic principles. My father-in-law has likewise savings in the bank, and we dare not venture to tell the old gentleman that his bank book is mere waste paper.

He is far from being a miser. It was only the other day he mentioned that he let interest and compound interest accumulate; we should find at his death that he had been really grateful for all our tender care of him. In very deed one requires to be as firmly grounded as I am in socialistic principles to stand such reverses without in the least losing heart.

CHAPTER VI.

ASSIGNMENT OF WORK.

THE union between Franz and Agnes is suddenly put off indefinitely. The police have to-day distributed the orders relating to the occupations of the people, which orders are based partly upon the registration lately made, and partly upon the plan organised by the Government for regulating production and consumption.

True, Franz is to remain a compositor, but, unfortunately, he can't stay in Berlin, but is sent to Leipsig. Berlin requires now hardly one-twentieth part of the number of compositors it formerly employed. None but absolutely reliable Socialists are allowed on the *Onward*. Now Franz, through some unguarded expressions in Palace Square over that unfortunate savings bank business, is regarded with some suspicion. Franz will have it, too, that politics have had something to do with the assignment of labour; and he says, for instance, that in Berlin the Younkers have been completely scattered as a party. One had to go as a paperhanger to Inowrazlaw because there was a scarcity of paperhangers there, whereas in

Berlin there are too many. Franz quite lost all patience, and said it seemed to him that the old law against the Socialists, with its expatriation, had come to life again. Well, we must excuse a little haste in an engaged young man who sees himself suddenly, and for an indefinite period, cut off from the girl of his heart.

I tried to offer Franz a little comfort by remarking that in the very next house a married couple had been separated by the action of this law. The wife goes to Oppeln in the capacity of nurse, the husband to Magdeburg as a bookkeeper. This set my wife going, and she wanted to know how anyone dared to separate husband and wife? It was infamous, and so on. The good soul entirely forgot that in our new community marriage is a purely private relationship, as Bebel lucidly explained in his book on woman. The marriage knot can at any time, and without the intervention of any official whatever, be tied and again untied. The Government is hence not at all in a position to know who is married, and who is not. In the registries of names we find therefore, as might be logically expected, that all persons are entered in their Christian names, and the maiden names of their mothers. In a well-considered organisation of production and consumption, the living together of married couples is clearly only practicable where the scale of occupation allows of such an arrangement; not *vice versâ*. It would never do to make the organisation of labour in any way dependent upon a private relationship which might be dissolved at any moment.

My wife reminded me that in old times appointments which were not quite agreeable to their holders had often been annulled, or exchanges made; we might anyhow make an effort to get Franz exchanged back to Berlin.

It occurred to me that an old friend and colleague whose acquaintance I had first made when in durance at Ploezensee, under the law against the Socialists, held now an influential position on the Labour Organisation Board. But on going there I found this department at the town hall besieged by hundreds of people who had come on a similar errand, and I was unable to obtain entrance to the room. Fortunately I encountered in the corridor another colleague who is on the same Board. I told him what we had so much at heart, but he advised me to let the grass grow a little over the part Franz had taken in the tumult in front of the palace, before applying for his removal back to Berlin.

I further took advantage of this opportunity to complain that although my choice of the bookbinder's craft had been confirmed, I was now no longer a master as formerly, but only a journeyman. But he told me there was really no help for this. It appears that in consequence of the system of doing everything on a large scale the demand for small masters is much less than ever it was before. He went on to say that in consequence of a big mistake having been discovered in an account, there would be a vote of credit brought in to appoint 500 controllers; and he advised me to apply for one of these posts, or to try for a place as public checker. I mean to follow his advice.

My wife's wishes have so far been acceded to that her services as attendant at one of the Children's Homes are accepted. But, unfortunately, she is not appointed to the one where our youngest born will

THE SOCIALISTIC FUTURE. 19

be. They say that, as a matter of principle, mothers can only receive appointments as nurses and attendants to such homes where their own children are not inmates. By this means it is intended to prevent any preference being shown to one's own children, and any jealousies which other mothers might feel. This certainly sounds very fair, but Paula cannot fail to feel the hardships of it. This is always the way with women, and they are so inclined to put their private wishes before State reasons.

Agnes is no longer to be a milliner, but has got an appointment as a seamstress. There will be no great demand for fine head-gear, or gew-gaws of any kind now. From all I hear the new scheme of supply aims solely at the production of all articles *en masse*. Hence it follows, as a matter of course, that there will be but a very limited demand for skilled labour, taste, and what more or less approaches to art in trade. But it is all the same to Agnes, and she says she doesn't care what they do with her so long as she can't share her lot with Franz. They forget, as I told them, that even Providence itself could not serve all alike to their full content. "Then they should have left each one to look after himself," interrupted Franz; "we could never have been so badly off under the old system."

In order to pacify them somewhat, I read to them out of the *Onward* a statement in tabular form dealing with the selections of trades people had made, and with the labour assignments to them. A greater number of persons had registered themselves as gamekeepers than there are hares within forty miles' circumference of Berlin. From the number of entries made the Government would have no difficulty in posting a hall-porter at every single door in Berlin: every tree could have its forester, every horse its groom. There are a great many more nurse-girls than kitchen-maids registered; more coachmen than ostlers. The number of young women who have put their names down as waitresses and public singers is very considerable, but this superabundance is balanced by the paucity of those who desire to become sick-nurses. There is no lack of salesmen and saleswomen. The same remark applies to inspectors, managers, foremen, and similar positions; there is even no scarcity of acrobats. The entries for the more arduous labours of the pavior, the stoker, the smelter are more sparse. Those who have manifested a desire to become cleansers of sewers are, numerically, not a strong body.

Under these circumstances, what has the Government to do in order to bring their scheme for organising production and consumption into some sort of harmony with the entries made by the people? Should Government attempt a settlement by fixing a lower rate of wages for those branches which showed any over-crowding, and a higher rate for those labours which were not so coveted? This would be a subversion of the fundamental principles of Socialism. Every kind of labour which is useful to the community (Bebel always taught) must appear of equal value in the eyes of the community. The receipt of unequal wages would soon tend to favour inequalities in the style of living; or it would enable the better paid ones to effect savings. By this latter means, and indirectly, in the course of time a capitalist class would grow up, and thus the whole socialistic system of production be thrown into disorder. Government had under its consideration the suggestion to effect a settlement of the difficulty by fixing working-days by varying lengths. The objection to this was that some violence must then inevitably be done to the natural and necessary dependence of various occupations upon each other. That matter of supply and demand, which played such a prominent part under the old reign of capital, is not to be suffered under any circumstances to come up again.

Government reserves to itself the right to direct criminals to do the more disagreeable kinds of work. It has furthermore adopted the counsel which Bebel used to give, *viz.*, that of allowing more variety of work to the same individual. Perhaps in the course of time we may see the same workmen, during different hours of the same day, engaged in the most diverse and manifold occupations.

For the present no other plan seemed feasible than that of a lottery. The entries for each trade were set apart by themselves, and from these entries the appointments required for each branch of trade by the Government organisation scheme were settled by a simple drawing of lots. Those who drew blanks in the first lottery cast lots again and again until they got a trade; and in this way the vacancies were filled up in these branches of labour for which there had been a scarcity of applicants. I understand that a kind of labour they do not at all relish has, in this way, fallen to the lot of a good many people.

Franz says there always have been horse-raffles and dog-raffles and all kinds of raffles, but this is the first time that man-raffles have taken place. He says that even at the very beginning the Government are so at their wits' end that they have to resort to a toss-up.

"But can't you see," I said to him, "that for the future all things are to be arranged on an entirely new and different basis? For the present we are still feeling the after effects of the old system of exploiting, and of the dominion of capital. Once let the spirit of Socialism be fully awakened, and enjoy universal sway, and you will find that the most arduous, disagreeable, and dangerous labours will be the very ones which will draw the greatest numbers of volunteers; and the reason is quite obvious. These volunteers will be sustained by the lofty consciousness that their labours are for the good of the public at large, and they will no longer have the reflection that they minister to the vile lust of gain of unprincipled plunderers."

But I could not get the young people to see things in this light.

CHAPTER VII.

NEWS FROM THE PROVINCES.

ALL young men of the age of twenty are required to enrol themselves within three days. Agnes' brother is among this number. The "National Bulwark," as it is called, is to be organised and armed with all speed. The spacious buildings of the War Ministry were to have been converted into a vast infant's school for the sake of the fine gardens adjoining. (This school was to have been, too, the scene of my wife's labours.) It is, however, now determined to leave things as they were.

The internal affairs of the country render it necessary that the National Bulwark should be called out earlier than had been intended, and also that the organisation be on a far larger scale than had been at first contemplated. The New Provincial Councillors are constantly sending urgent requests for military assistance to aid them in the work of establishing the new laws in country districts and in small towns Hence, it has been decided to establish at convenient centres all over the country, a battalion of infantry, a squadron of cavalry, and a battery. In order to ensure better security the troops are composed of men chosen from districts lying far asunder.

These country boors and louts must be brought to reason. They actually go the length of objecting to the nationalisation—or as the official term runs, the communalisation—of their private means, their possessions in the shape of acres, houses, cattle, farm stock and the like. Your small owner in the country will insist on remaining where he is, and sticking fast to what he has got, in spite of all you can tell him of the hard lot he has from sunrise to sunset. People of this sort could be left quietly where they are, but then the mischief is, it would greatly interfere with the vast scheme for the organisation of production. So there is no other way than to compel these thickheaded people by sheer force to see what is to their advantage. And when the whole organisation is once in full swing such persons will soon be convinced of the benefits that have been conferred upon them by Socialism.

Upon its becoming known that all the big landed estates and large farms had been declared State property, all farm servants and agricultural labourers at once attached themselves zealously to our side. But these people are now no longer content to remain where they were. A great desire for a change has come over them, and they all make for the larger towns, chiefly for Berlin. Here, in Frederick St., and *unter den Linden*, may now be seen daily the most outlandish-looking individuals from the remotest parts of the country. Many of them arrive with wives and families, and with the scantiest means. But they nevertheless clamour for food and drink, clothing, boots, and what not of the best and dearest. They had been told, they say, that everybody in Berlin lived on the fat of the land. I wish such were only really the case!

But, of course, we can't do with these backwoodsmen here, and they are to be bundled off back to where they came from, which will cause some little bitterness. It would be a pretty state of things if the magnificent scheme of the Government for regulating production and consumption were to be made sixes and sevens of in this fashion by a capricious wandering to and fro of people from the provinces. We should have them at one time swarming down like flights of locusts upon the stores accumulated here, to the neglect of necessary labours in their own parts; whilst at other times, when the fit took them not to come, we should behold all the stuff that had been got in in anticipation of their visit, spoiling on our hands.

It would unquestionably have been better if those regulations which have only just been issued had been issued at the very first. According to these regulations no one can now temporarily leave his place of residence without first providing himself with a leave-of-absence ticket; and no one can make

THE SOCIALISTIC FUTURE.

a permanent removal without receiving such directions from higher quarters. It is, of course, intended that Berlin shall still remain a much-visited capital; but people are not to come and go in a capricious, aimless way, but only, as the *Onward* simply and clearly sets forth, in a manner which shall accord with the carefully prepared calculations and plans of the Government. The socialistic State or, as we now say, the Community, is in earnest as respects the obligation on all persons alike to work; and it, therefore, is fully determined not to permit any vagabondism of any kind, not even any railway vagabondism.

Yesterday the Chancellor made another telling speech in that convincing manner which, as the *Onward* truly remarks, is so peculiarly his own. The question had been raised in the House whether an attempt should not be made to tranquillise the disaffected country districts by aggregating local possessions into local groups, instead of impounding such possessions for the benefit of the whole Community? These detached groups were to be called Local Produce Associations, each inhabitant of a district being a unit of the local group. "It is high time," said the Chancellor, in his speech, "that errors such as these —errors which reach back to the time of Lassalle, and which were fully disposed of at the Erfurt Conference of 1891—should be set at rest for ever. It is evident that the results of the establishment of various Local Produce Associations would be to introduce competition between the several associations. Then, again, the varying nature of the quality of the land must inevitably tend to produce gradations of prosperity and non-prosperity, and in this way to open a kind of back-door to the return of capital.

A well-digested scheme for the regulation of production and consumption, and an intelligent distribution of the craftsmen in each several department over the whole State, are things which cannot admit of any individualism, any competition, any personal or local independence. Socialism can never consent to do things by halves." (Loud applause.)

CHAPTER VIII.

THE LAST DAY TOGETHER.

I HAVE had rather a bad time of it to-day with my two women folk, my wife and Agnes. It was mother's birthday, a day whose return I have for the last twenty-five years greeted with joy. On the present occasion, alas! there was nothing but heaviness in our hearts. To-morrow Franz is to set out for Leipsig, and on the same day we must yield up our other two children. Grandfather is to remove into the Refuge for People of Advanced Years.

It will readily be understood that there was more thought of all these matters than of the birthday. My wife's heart was full to overflowing, especially at the sight of grandfather. "Socialism," said he, "is a calamity for all of us; I have foreseen this all along." I tried to comfort him by describing to him the easy, agreeable life he would lead at the Refuge.

"What is all that to me?" he cried, full of impatience. "When there I shall have to live and sleep and eat with strangers. I shall no longer have my daughter about me to look after me. I shall not be able to have my pipe whenever and wherever the humour takes me. I shall be no longer able to have games with Annie, or to listen to the tales Ernst brings home from school. I shall never hear how things are going on in your workshop. And whenever I become ill I shall be left quite to myself. Old trees should be left where they are, and never be transplanted. And I am sure the end won't be long in coming to me."

We tried to reassure him by promising to visit him very often.

"Such visits," said he, "are only a doing of things by halves. You are never alone and really at your ease, and you are constantly getting disturbed by other people."

We got little Annie, grandfather's pet, to do the best she could, in her confiding way, to solace him. The child was the only cheerful member of the company. Somebody had told her a lot of tales of all the cakes, pretty dolls, clever dogs, picture-books, and similar delights which were to be had at the Children's Homes. So she was never tired of talking of these things.

Franz manifests resignation, and quiet, firm resolution. But I don't like to see this in him. It looks to me as though he were devising some plans or other which he is determined not to betray. Whatever such plans may be I trust they are not at variance with our socialistic principles.

My second son, Ernst, does not much betray what his thoughts and feelings are. Towards his mother, however, he has been especially tender, and this as a general thing is not at all his way. We had meant to apprentice him to some trade now, and he had looked forward to this with much pleasure. He has a skilful hand, and would push his way onwards at a trade; but he has not made all the progress in school matters that one could have wished. But now it must be otherwise, as lads of his age, one and all, have to be kept at school a few years longer before they can receive a technical training.

Upon everyone of her birthdays mother treats us to a prime, juicy loin of veal, which Franz playfully calls our historical joint.

"When you come to see me, as I hope you will soon," said my wife, sadly, as the joint appeared on the table, "I shall not be able to set roast veal before you, for I shall then no longer have a kitchen of my own."

"I have the greatest respect imaginable for your roast joints," I replied; "but it would never do to give up our ideals on such grounds. So far from there being any lack of roast joints in the future we shall have them even more frequently than hitherto, and many another delicacy in addition."

"True enough," she answered; "but we shall not enjoy these things together. One gets his meals here, another there. The distress caused to the individual heart by all this tearing asunder is poorly compensated for by knowing that the public at large live better. I don't care a straw about the joint, but I do care about the social life of the family."

"Ah, I see," I said jocularly. "It is not for the sake of the pennyworth of cake, but only for the kind regards which accompany it. Never mind, old lady; rest assured we shall not have any the less regard for one another in the future, and we shall have more leisure to show it than we have had so far."

"Well, I am sure of one thing," she said. "I would a great deal rather work ten or twelve hours a day at home for you all, than eight hours for other people's children, who are nothing to me."

After a short silence, she asked, querulously: "What I want to know is, why must things be so?"

And Agnes, who always seconds my wife when she gets on to such subjects, repeated the question even more querulously. Whenever these two talk a duet there is very little chance left for me, especially when Franz remains neutral, or, what is worse still, keeps nodding approval to Agnes."

"Have you then so entirely forgotten those delightful lectures by Miss W.," I asked, "those lectures on the emancipation of women, and on the equality of women's rights in all respects with the rights of men? You found those lectures at the time as inspiring as Bebel's book."

"Oh, Miss W. is an old maid," they replied, "who has never had more than her one furnished room."

"She may none the less on that account be in the right," I answered. "The principle of equal rights, equal obligations, irrespective of sex, constitutes the basis of the socialistic Community. Our platform is the total independence of the wife from her husband, and this end is to be obtained by securing to women an equal and independent income for services done away from their own homes: no more household serfs, and no more slavish services on the part of wives or servants. Hence we endeavour to reduce all household work to a minimum by transferring this as far as possible to great central establishments conducted by the State. We must have no children and no elderly persons about the homes, so that these, by their varying number in different families, may again give rise to all the gradations of wealth and poverty. These are the doctrines which Bebel taught us."

"I daresay all that is very nicely and mathematically worked out," said grandfather; "but it can never bring happiness. And why not? Because humanity is something more than a flock of sheep."

"Grandfather is quite right," cried Agnes. And then she clasped Franz round the neck, and hung upon him, and said she never had the least wish to be emancipated from him.

Under these circumstances there was at once an end to all reasonable argument.

But, after all, I wish to-morrow, with all its partings, were well over.

CHAPTER IX.

THE GREAT MIGRATION.

In place of the cab which we had expected to fetch away grandfather and the children, a furniture-van pulled up before the house in the early morning. An official who accompanied it said that we had no occasion to move out before the evening; his instructions at present were merely to fetch the furniture.

"Fetch the furniture?" said my wife in amazement. "I thought that household goods were to remain private property."

"Certainly, my good woman," answered the man. "We are by no means instructed to take all the things away. All that the Community lays claim to is what is comprised in this list."

And he handed us the inventory we had had to

THE SOCIALISTIC FUTURE.   31

give in previously, and also showed us a copy of the *Onward*, with a bye-law of the Government, which we had somehow, in the agitation of the last few days, quite overlooked.

My wife remained like one petrified, and it was long before she could somewhat recover herself. The official was meantime very patient and civil, and did all he could to reconcile her to the necessity of the step.

"My good lady," he said, "where in the world are we otherwise to get such a quantity of furniture together as will be required for the many State establishments for the education of children, the care of old people, the nursing of the sick, the providing the people with meals, and so on?"

"Then why not go to rich people," my wife asked, "to people who have great big mansions stuffed as full as they can hold with the most beautiful furniture?"

"We do that as well," he replied, smirkingly. "In Zoological Gardens St., Victoria St., Regent St., and that district there is quite a procession of furniture-vans. All traffic for other vehicles than these has been stopped for the present. No one is to retain more than a couple of beds, and as much other furniture as he can stow away in two or three good-sized rooms. But even then we have not a sufficiency. Only just imagine, we have here alone over 900,000 persons below the age of twenty-one who have to be housed in Children's Homes and in schools. Then you have another 100,000 persons over sixty-five who have to be provided for at the Refuges. In addition to all this, there are to be ten times as many beds as heretofore in all the hospitals. Now tell me where are we to get all these things from, and not steal. And tell me further what would be the good of all these beds, and tables, and cabinets to you when granny yonder, the young gentleman here, and the little girl are no longer inmates of the house?"

My wife wanted, at least, to know what we should do when they all came to visit us.

"Well, you will still have six chairs left," was the reply.

"Yes, but I mean when they stay overnight?" my wife asked.

"There will be some difficulty about that, as you will find very little room at the new place!" he answered.

It now came out that my good wife had suffered her imagination to lead her into supposing that at the new distribution of residences we should, at the very least, receive a neat little villa somewhere at the West End, and be then able to furnish one or two spare rooms for our friends. I must say, though, that Paula never had any grounds for letting her imagination take these lofty flights, inasmuch as Bebel always taught that domestic affairs should be on as small and frugal a scale as possible.

Paula tried to find comfort in the thought that grandfather and the children would at least sleep in their own old beds at their new places. She had fully meant, in any case, to send the cosy easy-chair to the Refuge for her father's use.

But the official shook his head at this.

"That is not quite what is intended," he said. "The collected articles will be sorted out, and the best use consistent with fitness and harmony made of them. The furniture in these places would be somewhat of a motley character if each inmate were to bring his own lumber with him."

This only served to cause renewed lamentations. The easy-chair had been our last birthday present to grandfather. It was as good as new, and the old gentleman always found it so comfortable and easy. Little Annie's cot had been slept in by all the children, one after another. It had been relegated to the lumber attic, and brought down again, time after time, as occasion required. The large wardrobe, which we subsequently gave up to grandfather, had been amongst the very first things we had bought when we got married, and this we obtained by weekly payments. It took us no end of labour and economy to get our few things together. The looking-glass was a heirloom from my father. He always used to shave himself before it. I remember knocking off that bottom corner as a boy, and getting a good thrashing for it too. Thus, one way and another, a part of our very life's history clings to every piece of furniture about the place. And now all these things are to become mere broker's gear, and to be scattered for ever!

But our regrets were unavailing, and we had to let them load the van with our furniture. Towards evening another official came to fetch away grandfather and the children. But we were not permitted to accompany them, the official saying with some asperity, that there must be an end somewhere to all these partings. And I cannot say that the man was altogether in the wrong. The fact is, all this display of feeling is not quite in character with the victories of reason of modern times. Now that the reign of universal brotherhood is about beginning, and millions stand locked in a fond embrace, we must strive to let our gaze wander far beyond the petty narrow limits of past and vanquished times.

I tried to point this out to my wife when the others had all gone, and Paula and I were left alone. But oh, dear! it is dreadfully quiet and desolate in the half-empty rooms. We have never known quiet like this since the first year of our marriage.

"I wonder whether the children and grandfather will have good beds to-night!" my wife said presently. "And whether they will be able to sleep. Poor little Annie, indeed, was nearly asleep when the man came to fetch her. I wonder, too, whether her clothes have been delivered all right, and whether they have put her long night-gown on, so that she won't take cold. The child has such a way of kicking the coverlet off in her sleep. I had laid her night-dress quite on the top of the other things, with a little note for the attendant."

I fear we shall, neither of us, be able to sleep a wink to-night. It is only by degrees that one can get used to these things.

CHAPTER X.

THE NEW CURRENCY.

TRADE is very brisk with the photographers. All persons between the ages of twenty-one and sixty-five years, that is to say, all those who are not inmates of State establishments, have received instructions to have their likenesses taken. This step is an essential part of the Government plan for the introduction of the new currency. The old system of bank-notes and coins is to be abolished, and so-called money certificates issued instead.

In a leading article on this innovation, the *Onward* very truly remarks that the Minister of Exchange has displayed much sagacity and prudence in solving the problem of procuring a means of exchange which shall fulfil all the legitimate duties of such a medium, and at the same time not allow of the resuscitation of a capitalist class. Unlike gold and silver, the new currency possesses no intrinsic value, but it consists simply of orders or cheques drawn on the State as the sole possessor of all articles of sale.

Every labourer in the service of the State receives once a fortnight a series of money certificates in the form of a coupon booklet. The name of each holder is printed on the cover, and with a view to preventing the use of the coupons by other persons, it is enacted that the photograph of every individual holder be attached to his book of coupons. It is evident that the Government orders regulating the hours of labour for all persons alike, and prescribing for all persons the same scale of remuneration, will prevent the return of social inequalities consequent upon the gradations of faculty possessed by different people, and the use made of these faculties. But, in addition to this, care must be taken to prevent, through inequalities in the scale of consumption, all accumulations of value in the hands of such persons as are of a thrifty turn, or whose requirements are small. This was a self-evident danger, and, if disregarded, would in due time have the effect of producing a capitalist class, which would, by degrees, bring into subjection those less thrifty persons who were in the habit of consuming all their income.

To obviate the misappropriation and misuse of money certificates, it is expressly understood that coupons are not, under any circumstances, to be detached by the holders, but that they only then have their representative value when detached by the State vendors or other similar officials appointed for this purpose.

All payments are to be made on the spot in coupons. Thus, for instance, it is the business of the hall porter, stationed in each house, to detach daily a dwelling's coupon from the booklet of each person resident in the house.

The new distribution of dwellings is to take place immediately before the opening of the State cookshops, an arrangement by which the further necessity for private kitchens will be obviated. When these are opened, the equivalent for a dinner will be detached by the Government official in the shape of a dinner coupon; that for the allowance of bread (one pound and a half daily, per head), in the shape of a bread coupon, and so on. The several coupons in the booklets represent, of course, different values, very considerable latitude being left to the taste of each holder as to how he likes to employ his coupons. All purchases are to be made at the State magazines and shops, and care is to be taken that the vendors in every case detach none but coupons of exactly the right value.

As each coupon bears the same number as the outside cover, and every holder is entered in the Government registry, it is an easy matter at any time to learn from the collected coupons the way in which each person has expended his income. The Government is thus, at any moment, in a position to observe whether persons spend their income on dress, or on eating and drinking, or how they spend it; and knowledge of this kind must materially lessen the difficulty of regulating production and consumption.

Every purchaser has the fullest liberty either to apply to his own use such wares as he has obtained in exchange for coupons, or to resign them to the use of other persons. Nay, he may even bequeath things to others. The calumny that has often been hurled at Socialism, that it aims at the distinction of all private property, is thus, as the *Onward* pointedly shows, fully refuted, and refuted in a manner that ought to make the enemies and calumniators of Socialism blush with shame. Socialism never wished for more than to see such bounds set to individual caprice as should prevent the formation of private capital, and of a system of plundering.

Those persons who, at the expiration of the fortnight, have not used up all their coupons, get the remnant entered to their credit in the new booklet. But, of course, even here it is necessary to draw the line somewhere, and to concert measures to prevent these successive remnants heaping themselves up to actual capital. A sum of sixty marks is regarded as being more than sufficient to enable its possessor to indulge himself in the gratification of all reasonable desires. Any more considerable savings than sixty marks are forfeited to the State.

CHAPTER XI.

THE NEW DWELLINGS.

THE universal dwelling-house lottery has taken place, and we are now in possession of our new home; but

I cannot exactly say that we have bettered our position. We used to live S.W., at the front of the house, on the third storey. Oddly enough, a dwelling has fallen to our lot on the very same premises, only it happens to be at the back of the house, and quite in the back-yard, in fact. It is likewise on the third storey. My wife's disappointment is considerable. She had given up all thought of a small villa, but she still clung to the hope of getting a neat suite of rooms on an elegant flat.

I have always been rather choice in the matter of having a nice home. Hitherto we have had two good-sized rooms, two smaller ones, and the kitchen, for our family of six persons. True, the two smaller chambers in which grandfather and the children used to sleep can now be dispensed with, and the kitchen is now no longer a necessary part of a dwelling, inasmuch as the State cookshops are on the eve of being opened. But I had none the less ventured to hope that at least two or three neat and pretty rooms would fall to our share; but instead of this, we have got only a small room with one window, and a little poky garret similar to those in which servants used to sleep. The rooms are, too, somewhat darker and lower than our old ones. This is the whole extent of the accommodation.

Not that I would by any means convey that there has been the least unfairness. Our municipal body is quite straightforward, and none but rogues can give more than they are possessed of. It was set forth only yesterday, at a meeting of the Council, that our city has only one million rooms for its two millions of inhabitants. But the demand for space for various public and benevolent purposes has, in the socialistic

THE SOCIALISTIC FUTURE. 39

Community, immensely increased, and the space hitherto employed for such purposes only suffices to cover a small fraction of the present requirements. In the first place, room had to be found, in schools and various houses of maintenance, for a million of people, young and old. Furthermore, accommodation has been provided in hospitals for 80,000 people.

But it is clear that such public interests must take precedence of private ones. Hence it is only natural and right that the best and largest houses, more particularly at the West End, have been appropriated to these purposes. In the inner city, shops and magazines are crowded together, and many of the basements of these are fitted up as State cookshops for the million inhabitants who are not consigned to public institutions. Back-yard premises in suitable situations are being adapted as central wash-houses for this million. It will thus be seen that the setting apart of so much separate space for separate purposes has had the effect of materially curtailing the accommodation for private dwellings.

At the commencement of the new regime it was found, as already stated, that in round numbers one million rooms were at the disposal of the authorities. Of these, after deducting the requirements of the various public institutions, some 600,000 more or less smallish rooms remain, to which, however, must be added several hundred thousand kitchens (now become superfluous), attics, and garrets. As there are one million persons to provide for, it is at once seen that the space allotted is about one room per head; and in order to observe the utmost impartiality in the disposal of these rooms, they were assigned by lottery, each person from the age of twenty-one to sixty-five years, irrespective of gender, receiving a lottery ticket. And, indeed, this system of raffling is an excellent means of regulating the principle of equality wherever the essential features are disproportionate. The social democrats in Berlin, even under the old regime, had introduced this system of raffling for seats at the theatres.

Upon the completion of this casting lots for residences, exchanges of the rooms that had fallen to the various ticket-holders were permissible. Those persons who desired to remain together, such as married couples, for instance, but who had got their quarters in different streets, houses, or storeys, were allowed to exchange as best they could. For my part, I had to put up with a tiny room, a mere cupboard of a place, adjoining the room which had fallen to my wife's lot, and, in order to get this cupboard, I had to give up my nice room in a neighbouring house to a young man to whom the cupboard had fallen; but the main thing, after all, is that we do not get separated.

Not that all married couples have, by any means, yet been successful in obtaining a satisfactory exchange of rooms. There may be even some who do not take any particular pains to secure this end. Marriage is a private affair; and, therefore, officially, there can be no lotteries of larger dwellings for married people, and of smaller ones for those who are single. Were such the case, then, the termination of a marriage contract, for instance (which ought to be attainable at any moment), might have to be put off until single rooms for the individuals concerned were procurable. As it now is, each compound dwelling formed by the two halves to a marriage contract can, at a moment's notice, on the termination of the contract, be resolved into its original halves. All you have to do is to make a division of the furniture, and the thing is settled.

Thus we see that everything in the new Community has been settled in a logical and sagacious manner. All the arrangements guarantee full personal liberty to every man and every woman ; and how humiliated must those feel who used to maintain that Socialism meant the subjugation of the individual will.

Not that considerations of the above kind are personally of any moment to my better half and me; whether happiness or sorrow comes we shall stick together to the end of life's journey.

On our removal here we had, unfortunately, to leave a number of our things behind us. The new quarters were too small to stow away even the remnant that had been left to us after the day of the furniture-vans. As a matter of course, we have stuffed our little place as full as it will hold, so that we can scarcely move about. But the fact is, this old servant's closet of mine is so wretchedly small that it is precious little that I can get into it. It has fared no better with numerous persons. At the general removal vast numbers of things were left standing in the streets, for the simple reason that their owners could find no room for them in their new dwellings. These things were collected and carted away in order to augment as far as possible the still sparse outfit of the numerous public institutions.

However, we do not allow this to distress us in the least. The problem is to supersede the old-fashioned system of limited and meagre private existences, and to organise, in the new society, the life of the general public on such a vast and grand scale that all those bodily and mental good things, which were once only enjoyed by a favoured class, shall now be within the reach of everybody. The opening of the State cookshops to-morrow is to be followed by the opening of the new popular theatres.

CHAPTER XII.

THE NEW STATE COOKSHOPS.

It was, indeed, a wonderful achievement that to-day, in Berlin, one thousand State cookshops, each one capable of accommodating 1,000 persons, should have been opened at one stroke. True, those persons who had imagined that it would be like the *table d'hôte* of the great hotels of the past days, where a pampered upper class continually revelled in every refinement of culinary art—such persons, I say, must feel some little disappointment. As a matter of course, we have here likewise no trim, swallow-tailed waiters, no bills of fare a yard long, and no such paraphernalia.

In the State cookshops everything, even to the smallest details, has been anticipated and settled beforehand. No one person obtains the smallest preference over others. The picking and choosing amongst the various State cookshops cannot, of course, be tolerated. Each person has the right to dine at the cookshop of the district in which his dwelling is situated. The chief meal of the day is taken between 12 o'clock and 6 in the evening. Everyone has to report himself at the cookshop of his district, either during the mid-day rest or at the close of the day.

I am sorry to say that I can now no longer take my meals with my wife except on Sundays, as I have been accustomed to do for the last twenty-five years, inasmuch as our hours of labour are now entirely different.

Upon entering the dining-room an official detaches the dinner coupon from your book of money certificates, and hands you a number which indicates your turn. In the course of time others get up and go away, and your turn comes, and you fetch your plate of victuals from the serving tables. The strictest order is maintained by a strong body of police present. The police to-day—their number has now been augmented here to 12,000—rather gave themselves airs of importance in the State cookshops, but the fact is, the crowd was a very big one. It seems to me that Berlin proves itself to be on too small a scale for the vast undertakings of Socialism.

As each one takes his place just as he comes from his work the groups sometimes have a somewhat motley appearance. Opposite to me to-day sat a miller, and his neighbour was a sweep. The sweep laughed at this more heartily than the miller. The room at the tables is very cramped, and the elbows at each side hinder one much. However, it is not for long, the minutes allowed for eating being very stingily measured. At the expiration of the meagrely apportioned minutes—and a policeman with a watch in his hand stands at the head of each table to see that time is strictly kept—you are remorselessly required to make room for the next.

It is an inspiring thought to reflect that in every

State cookshop in Berlin on one and the same day exactly the same dishes are served. As each establishment knows how many visitors it has to count upon, and as these visitors are saved all the embarrassment of having to choose from a lengthy bill of fare, it is clear that no time is lost; whilst there is also none of that waste and loss consequent upon a lot of stuff being left, which circumstance used so much to enhance the price of dining at the restaurants of the upper classes. Indeed, this saving may well be reckoned amongst the most signal triumphs of the socialistic organisation.

From what a neighbour of ours, who is a cook, tells us, it had originally been intended to serve up various dishes on the same day. It soon appeared, however, that there would be a manifest want of equality in such an arrangement; inasmuch as those persons who, from any reason, were prevented from coming in good time would not have the chance of dining off such dishes as were "off," but would have to take whatever was left.

All the portions served out are of the same size. One insatiable fellow to-day who asked for more was rightly served by being heartily laughed at ; for what more deadly blow could be levelled at one of the fundamental principles of equality? For the same reason the suggestion to serve out smaller portions to women was at once indignantly rejected. Big, bulky men have to put up with the same sized portions, and to do as best they can. But, then, for such amongst them who, in their former easy circumstances, used to stuff themselves, this drawing in of their belt is quite a good and wholesome thing. For the rest people can bring with them from their homes as much bread as they like, and eat it with their meals. Furthermore, any persons who find their portions larger than they care for are not prohibited from giving a part to their neighbours.

According to what our neighbour the cook says, it appears that the Ministry of Public Nourishment has grounded its bill of fare on the experience gathered by scientific research as to the number of grains of nitrogenous matter and of hydro-carbonaceous matter that it is necessary to introduce into the body in order to keep the same intact. Each person's daily portion is about one-third of a pound of meat, with either rice, groats, or some vegetable or other, to which is generally added a plentiful supply of potatoes. On Thursdays we get sauerkraut and peas. Posters announce what is to be cooked on each day, and these posters give you the bill of fare for the whole week, just as they used to announce the plays at the theatres for the entire week.

Where, I should like to know, in the whole world, has there ever been a people every individual of which was assured, day by day, of his portion of flesh-meat, as is now the case with us? Even a king of France, ruminating once on such matters, could form to himself no higher ideal than that on Sundays every peasant should have his fowl in the stew-pan. Then, too, we must remember that outside the system of nourishment provided by the State it is left to the taste of everybody to treat himself to whatever he fancies both in the morning and evening—that is to say, provided it be within the bounds of the money certificate.

No more poor, starving, wretched, homeless creatures! For every man, as the day comes round, his portion of beef! The thought of having attained such ends as these is so inspiring that one can readily pardon any trifling inconveniences which the new system has brought with it. True, the portions of meat would be none the worse for being a little larger, but then our circumspect Government adopted the wise plan of not dealing out, at the commencement, more meat than had previously on an average been consumed here. Later on these things will all be different, and in process of time, when the new arrangements shall have more and more approached completion, and the period of transition is past, we shall have everything on a vaster and more magnificent scale.

But there is one thing which hinders my pinions taking the lofty flight they otherwise would, and that is the concern which my good wife shows. She is become very nervous, and her state gets worse day by day. During all the twenty-five years of our married life we have never had so many painful scenes and explanations as since the beginning of the new era. The State cookshops, too, are not a bit to her taste. The food, she says, is barracks' rations, and a poor substitute for the wholesome fare people used to have at their own homes. She complains of the meat being done too much, of the broth being watery, and so on. She says, too, that she at once loses all appetite by knowing beforehand what she has to eat during a whole week. And yet how often she had complained to me that, with the high prices of things, she was at her wits' end to know what to cook. Formerly she was rejoiced, when we now and then took a day's excursion, to think she was released for that day from the bother of cooking anything. Well, this is the way with women, and they always have something to say against whatever they have not had a hand in cooking. My hope is, however, as soon as my wife shall have paid visits to the children and her father at the Benevolent Institutions, and have found them hearty and contented, that that equanimity will be restored to her which in old times never deserted her even in our severest trials.

CHAPTER XIII.

A VEXING INCIDENT.

OUR Chancellor is not made so much of as he used to be. I am sorry to see this, because it is impossible to find anywhere a more capable, energetic, and active State leader, or a more thorough and consistent Socialist. But, then, it is not everybody who is as unbiased as I am. There are a great many people who don't quite care for the new order of things, or who are somewhat disappointed in their expectations; and all these persons lay the blame on the Chancellor. This is especially the case with women since the universal removals and the introduction of the State cookshops. There is even talk of a party of re-action being formed amongst women, but I am thankful to say my wife is not of this number, and I hope to goodness that Agnes is not.

The report has been assiduously circulated against the Chancellor that he is at heart an aristocrat. It is even said that he does not clean his boots himself, that he suffers a servant to brush and clean his clothes, that he sends someone from the Treasury to fetch his meals from the State cookshop of his district, instead of going there himself. Such things would, indeed, be grave offences against the principle of equality; but it is a question, after all, whether the charges are true.

Anyhow, this dissatisfaction which has clearly been nourished by the Younkers, a party composed mainly of flighty youths for whom nothing is good enough, has just culminated in an outburst of public feeling which was manifested in a very blameworthy and ugly spirit. The unveiling of the new allegorical monument in commemoration of the great deeds of the Paris Commune of 1871, took place yesterday in the square, which was formerly Palace Square. Since then the square has been continually beset by crowds anxious to view this magnificent monument. Returning from a carriage-drive, the Chancellor had to pass the square. He had almost reached the entrance to the Treasury, when all at once, from the neighbourhood of the Arsenal, hissing, shouts, and general tumult ensued. In all probability the mounted police (which is now re-instated), had shown rather too great zeal in procuring a passage for the Chancellor's carriage. The tumult increased in fury, and there were cries: "Down with the aristocrat; down with the proud upstart; pitch the carriage into the canal! The crowd evidently felt greatly irritated at the now rare spectacle of a private carriage.

The Chancellor, with ill-concealed anger, nevertheless bowed courteously in all directions, and gave orders to drive on slowly. All at once, however, he was saluted by a lot of mud and dirt which emanated seemingly from a group of women, and I saw him free himself, as far as possible, from this dirt, and noticed, too, that he forbade the police to attack the women with their truncheons. Scenes such as this, and which are totally unworthy of Socialism, certainly ought not to occur. And I have been glad to hear to-day, from various quarters, that it is intended to prepare great ovations for the Chancellor.

CHAPTER XIV.

A MINISTERIAL CRISIS.

THE Chancellor has tendered his resignation. All well-intentioned persons must sincerely regret this step, especially after yesterday's event. But the Chancellor is said to be in an overwrought and nervous state. And, indeed, this can scarcely be wondered at, for he has had a hundred times more thought and work than any chancellor under the old system had. The ingratitude of the mob has deeply wounded him, and the incident of yesterday was just the last drop which has made the cup run over.

It has come out, however, that the boot cleaning question was really at the bottom of the ministerial crisis. It is now known that the Chancellor some little time back handed over to the Cabinet an elaborate memorandum, which memorandum, however, the other ministers always contrived to persistently shelve. The Chancellor insists now on attention being paid to his memorandum, and he has had it inserted in the *Onward*. He demands that class differences be instituted, and says that for his part he cannot possibly dispense with the services of others. The maximum eight hours' day simply cannot and does not exist for a chancellor, nor could otherwise exist than by having three chancellors to govern in shifts of eight hours each of the twenty-four. He urges that he, as Chancellor, lost a lot of valuable time each morning over cleaning his boots, brushing his clothes, tidying up his room, fetching his breakfast, and similar offices; and that, as a consequence, matters of grave State import, which he alone was in a position to attend to, were subjected to vexing delay. He had no other choice, he says, than either to appear occasionally before the ambassadors of friendly powers minus a button or two on his coat, or to, himself, (the Chancellor, as is well known, is not married,) do such small repairs as were too pressingly urgent, or too trifling, to be sent to the great State repairing shops. He argues further that by having a servant to perform such little offices much valuable time would have been saved to the public. Then again the having to take his meals at the one appointed State cookshop was very irksome, by reason of the crowd of suppliants who daily organised a hunt after him. As for his carriage-drives, he never took them except when, from the limited time at his disposal, it was otherwise quite impossible to obtain a mouthful of fresh air.

All this sounds, of course, very plausible, but there is no denying that a proposition of this kind is diametrically opposed to the principle of social equality, and that it would only too strongly tend to introduce the system of household slavery once more. That which is demanded by the Chancellor for himself others might with equal right demand, and we should soon have his colleagues in the Cabinet, and others, such, for instance, as heads of Government departments, directors of the numerous State institutions, mayors of towns, etc. etc., making the same pretensions. On the other hand, however, it certainly does seem a pity that the whole vast machinery of the State, upon whose smooth working such mighty issues depend, should now and then come to a stop because the Chancellor has to sew a button on, or to polish his boots before he can receive someone in audience.

This is a question of greater moment than is apparent to everyone at first sight. But that such an excellent Chancellor, and such a consistent Socialist should in the course of his career be tripped up by a stumbling-block of this kind cannot be too much regretted.

CHAPTER XV.

EMIGRATION.

THE ministerial crisis called forth by the boot-polishing question is not yet over. Meantime, a decree has been issued against all emigration without the permission of the authorities. Socialism is founded upon the principle that it is the duty of all persons alike to labour, just as under the old regime the duty to become a soldier was a universally recognised one. And just as in the old days young men who were ripe for military service were never allowed to emigrate without authority, so can our Government similarly not permit the emigration from our shores of such persons as are of the right age to labour. Old persons who are beyond work, and infants, are at liberty to go away, but the right to emigrate cannot be conceded to robust people who are under obligations to the State for their education and culture, so long as they are of working age.

At the beginning of the new order of things scarcely

any other persons than gentlemen of private means, with their families, showed any desire to get across the borders. True, the working powers of these people had been originally taken account of as a factor in the general sum; but it soon turned out that the labour done by such persons as had never been accustomed to harder work than cutting off coupons, or signing receipts, was of such little value that further assistance from these quarters could well be dispensed with. These people were hence quite at liberty to go. The main thing was to take care that they did not take money or money's worth with them over the frontier. Then again, the emigration of nearly all the painters, sculptors, and authors was a thing that could be viewed with the most perfect equanimity. The new system of working on a grand scale, and more or less on one and the same pattern, was not at all to the taste of these gentlemen. They raised objections to working with others in the great State workshops, for the good of the State in general, and to being subjected to the supervision of officials. Let all such malcontents go! We shall have no lack of poets, who, in their leisure hours, will gladly sing the praises of Socialism. It had been intimated to artists and sculptors that they would no longer be able to lay their works of art at the feet of insolent wealthy upstarts, but would have in future to dedicate them to the nation at large. And that does not at all suit these servants of Mammon.

There is, however, one unpleasant fact in connection with the emigration of all the sculptors, and that is, that the proposed erection of statues to many of the departed heroes of our cause seems to be delayed indefinitely. Not even the statues of those memorable pioneers Stadthagen and Liebknecht are completed. On the other hand, the clearance of the salons of the bourgeoisie has placed a vast amount of sculpture at our disposal for the decoration of our meeting-halls and the like.

A word as to authors. These gentlemen who criticise everything, and whose very business it is to spread discontent amongst the people, may, in fact, readily be dispensed with in a State where the will of the masses is law. Long ago Liebknecht used those memorable words: "He who does not bend to the will of the majority, he who undermines discipline must be bundled out."

If all such gentlemen go of their own accord so much the better.

If this had been all, no prohibition of emigration had ever been needed. But the incomprehensible part of the business is that it was observed that useful people, and people who had really learnt something, went away in ever-increasing numbers to Switzerland, to England, to America, in which countries Socialism has not succeeded in getting itself established. Architects, engineers, chemists, doctors, teachers, managers of works and mills, and all kinds of skilled workmen, emigrated in shoals. The main cause of this would appear to be a certain exaltation of mind which is greatly to be regretted. These people imagine themselves to be something better, and they cannot bear the thought of getting only the same guerdon as the simple honest day labourer. Bebel very truly said: "Whatever the individual man may be, the Community has made him what he is. Ideas are the product of the Zeitgeist in the minds of individuals."

Unfortunately the Zeitgeist under the old system long went wandering about, lost in the mazes of error. Hence all these mad notions about the superiority of one man over another.

As soon as our young people shall have received proper training in our socialistic institutions, and shall have become penetrated with the noble ambition to devote all their energies to the service of the Community, so soon shall we be well able to do without all these snobs and aristocrats. Until such time, however, it is only right and fair that they should stay here with us.

Under these circumstances the Government is to be commended for stringently carrying out its measures to prevent emigration. In order to do so all the more effectually, it has been deemed expedient to send strong bodies of troops to the frontiers, and to the seaport towns. The frontiers towards Switzerland have received especial attention from the authorities. It is announced that the standing army will be increased by many battalions of infantry and squadrons of cavalry. The frontier patrols have strict instructions to unceremoniously shoot down all fugitives.

Our Chancellor is an energetic man, and it is to be hoped he will long continue at the head of affairs.

CHAPTER XVI.

RETIREMENT OF THE CHANCELLOR.

My ardent wish has not been fulfilled. The Chancellor's resignation has been accepted, and the President of the Chamber has been nominated as his successor. It seems the Cabinet was not able to come to a unanimous determination to accept the responsibility of allowing the Chancellor to engage a few servants for his private convenience. The chief ground for this was, that such an infraction of the principle of social equality would lead to altogether incalculable consequences. Hence the necessity for the reconstruction of the Cabinet. Let us bear in mind the danger we should run of causing the whole socialistic edifice to come tumbling about our ears if only one single essential key-stone were once tampered with. It was in reference to this very identical question of boot-cleaning that Bebel once wrote: " No man is degraded by work, not even when that work consists of cleaning boots. Many a man of high birth has had to find this out in America."

The Government was strongly inclined to follow the method proposed by Bebel for the solution of this difficulty in practical life, by turning increased attention to the question of getting clothes brushed and boots cleaned by means of machinery. But the prospect of having to wait for suitable machinery to do all such offices for him did not seem at all to the Chancellor's taste, so he has retired from office.

His successor is stated to be of a more conciliatory, but less energetic, character; a man who is determined not to be obnoxious in any quarter, but to make matters pleasant all round.

With somewhat too much ostentation, the new Chancellor appeared to-day at the State cookshop of his district, duly taking his place in the long row, and dining when it came to his turn. Afterwards he was to be seen, *Unter den Linden*, with a large bundle of old clothes under his arm, which he was taking to the district repairing-shop to have cleaned and repaired.

CHAPTER XVII.

IN AND ABOUT THE WORKSHOPS.

I AM very glad that I have now received the appointment as checker which my friend in office promised me some time ago. I shall no longer have to be employed in the workshop. I only wish Franz had the same good luck, and could get away from his compositor's desk. Not for one moment that we are above our trades, but I know that Franz feels exactly as I do, and the style in which work is now done in all workshops does not suit Franz and me a bit. One does not work merely for the sake of a bit of bread, and nothing more. Schiller was one of the bourgeois, but notwithstanding this, I always liked those lines of his:

> " 'Tis this indeed mankind doth grace,
>   (And hence the gift to understand,)
> First in his inward self to trace
> All that he fashions with his hand."

Unfortunately, our mates in the workshops nowadays are not conscious of any such feeling. So far is this from being the case that anybody would think workshops are simply places to kill time in, and nothing more. The universal watchword is:

> " Don't push on too fast,
>   Lest the laggards be last."

Piece-work and working in gangs have ceased

This is only natural, as such styles of working could never be brought into harmony with the ideas of equality of wages and of working hours. But what Franz does not quite like, as he writes me, is the way they have now of spinning the work out so. In spite of sure and regular wages, they say:

"If the job is not finished to-day it will be finished to-morrow."

Diligence and zeal are looked upon as stupidity and perversity. And indeed why should one be industrious? The most diligent comes off no better than the laziest. No one is any longer, so writes Franz, the forger of the links of his own happiness, but others forge the links which shall fetter you just as it pleases them.

This is the strain in which Franz writes, and this time he is not so much in the wrong as he usually is.

There is no describing the amount of damage done to material and tools through inattention and carelessness. It would have driven me crazy if, when I was a master, I had been plagued with such a crew of workmen as I now have to work with. The other day it got rather too much for me, and, my patience being exhausted, I made a little appeal to them in these words:

"Colleagues, the Community expects every man to do his duty. We have only eight hours' work. You are all old Socialists, and you will remember the hope Bebel used to have that, when the new order of things came, the pure moral atmosphere would stimulate every man to excel his neighbour. Only just reflect, comrades, that we no longer toil for capitalists and plunderers, but for the Community. And everyone of us gets back a part of whatever benefit the Community reaps as a whole."

"Fine preaching!" they said mockingly. "It is a pity we have no longer occasion for parsons. Bebel promised us a four hours' day, and not an eight hours' one. The Community is a large affair. Shall I work and slave for the 50 millions whilst the other 49,999,999 take it easy? What could I buy myself with this one fifty-millionth part of the fruit of my additional industry, supposing I were really to get it back?"

And then they all sang in chorus:

"Is our Community not to thy taste?
Get thee gone to another with all possible haste."

Since that, I have, of course, not said another word. Franz has had experiences similar to mine. The newspaper in their office is hardly ever ready for going to press at the right time, although they have half as many compositors again on it as in old times. The longer the night the greater the quantity of beer which is drunk during work, and the greater the number of printers' errors.

Lately the foreman was unwell, and Franz had to take his place for a day or two. Franz on one occasion respectfully asked the others to make a little less noise, and upon this the whole body struck up the "Marseillaise," taking care to especially emphasize the words, "Down with despotism."

There are still masters and foremen in the workshops just as there were formerly, only with this difference, that they are now chosen by the workmen. When no longer acceptable to the workmen they are deposed. Hence they have to take care to keep in with the leaders in a shop, and with the majority. Those persons who, like Franz and myself, do not altogether go with the masses, are in rather a bad fix. At one time they get badly treated by the masters, and at another by the mates. And the worst of it is, you can no more get away from such a workshop than a soldier can escape from the company in which his drill-sergeant ill-treats him.

The late Chancellor foresaw all this well enough, but he was unable to alter it. The list of penalties enacted under his leadership against all infractions of the duty of labour is to be seen in all workshops where it has not yet been torn down. In this list penalties are threatened against idleness, inattention, disobedience, carelessness, impertinence to superiors, and a host of offences. These penalties consist of the withdrawal of the money-certificate, the reduction of the meat rations, the deprivation of the entire midday meal, and even of incarceration. But where there is none to bring a charge there is no need of a judge.

Directors and managers are chosen just in the same way as masters and foremen, and they have to look to it that they do not ruffle those who elect them.

In those rare cases where denunciations do take place, the judicial proceedings are tedious, and full of detail. Recently, however, a number of builders got denounced by passers-by, who had their patience tired out by the lengthy intervals of rest taken, and by the careful scrutiny applied to every individual brick. On another occasion, the inmates of an entire establishment were transferred to another part of the country. But, as a rule, this transference to other parts only arises from political reasons. It is on this account that the Younkers are now agitating to obtain for all working-men the same permanence which judges enjoy in their office.

This matter of removal to other places has its odd side. The principle of social equality requires that every man, no matter where he be, finds everything precisely as it was in the old place. He finds exactly the same wages, the same food, the same dwelling, and so on, as those he left behind him.

Well, Rome was not built in a day. And this very spirit of selfishness which we see so much of in our workshops, what is it other than the evil inheritance left us by a state of society in which every man strove to gain an advantage over every other man? Our new schools and institutions will very soon create that "moral atmosphere" in which the tree of Socialism will grow and flourish, and extend the welcome shadow of its branches to the whole human species.

CHAPTER XVIII.

FAMILY MATTERS.

SUNDAY was such a Sunday as I had never spent before. My wife got permission at last to visit little Annie. It seems that the observance of order in the Children's Homes necessitates the regulation that parents should only see their children in their due turn. How my wife had pictured to herself the meeting with her child! All sorts of cakes, and sweetmeats, and playthings had been got together to take to her. But to mother's great distress she found she had to leave all these things behind her at the entrance. It was forbidden, she learned, for any of the children to have any playthings which were not common to all, because this would not accord with their education, which taught absolute social equality. The same thing applied to sweetmeats. Such things were only too apt to give rise to quarrels and vexations, and to disturb the regular course of matters in the Home.

My wife was in perfect ignorance of these new regulations, as for some time past she has been engaged in the kitchen of her Home, and not in attending to the children.

Then again, my wife had expected that Annie would show more lively and tender delight at meeting with her mother. But in her new surroundings the child was disposed to be less confiding than she had always been. True, the separation had not been a long one, but there is a good deal of truth in the case of young children, in the words, "Out of sight out of mind." Then again, the idea of seeing her mother had constantly been associated in Annie's mind with the expectation of sweets and playthings. But now she beheld her mother come with empty hands. Childlike, she soon wanted a change again, and she quickly got away from the embraces of her mother in order to rejoin the other children at play.

My wife found Annie looking somewhat pale and changed. This is probably due to the different way of living, and the different kind of nourishment. Naturally, the strictest order is maintained in the Home. But (and the same intention pervades all our institutions) there is no superfluity of victuals, and the large scale of the undertaking does not admit of any pampering of individual children. Children's looks vary so rapidly, and were Annie now at home with us, her looks would hardly disquieten the experienced mother. But, of course, it is a different thing altogether when separated, and mother now pictures to herself the approach of some disease which she sees herself powerless to contend against.

A conversation my wife had with one of the Kindergarten teachers of the Home threw her into considerable agitation. My wife was lamenting the separation of young children from their parents, when this person cut short her complaint by the abrupt remark:

"Oh, we hear these doleful complaints here daily. Even animals, devoid of reason, soon get over it when their young are taken away. With how much more ease ought women to become reconciled to it, women who are reckoned amongst thinking beings."

My wife wanted to complain to the governor of this woman's unfeelingness, but I advised her not to do so, because the woman would be sure to have her revenge out of Annie. She does not know what it is to be a mother. And she can't even get a husband, although, as I am credibly informed, it is not for lack of having, on several occasions, made use of the equality now enjoyed by women of themselves proposing.

Before my wife had returned from the long journey to the Children's Home, grandfather came in. It was with difficulty that the old gentleman had found his way up the steep and dark staircase to our new home. I was really thankful that my wife was not present, because her father's complaints would only have made her heart still heavier.

To say the truth, they were trifling and external matters he had to complain about. But then, old people have this weakness of clinging to old habits and little ways, and in the maintenance houses all such little things are, with some harshness, broken through and swept away. Grandfather fancies, too, his health is not quite so good as it used to be. Now he has a pain here, anon he feels a pinching or a pricking sensation there, and is often out of sorts. Externally I saw no difference in him, but the fact is, grandfather has now a good deal more time to think about himself than he had in our family circle, where there was always something to interest him and distract his attention. He used to be a good deal in the workshop with me, and here he would try to make himself useful. What he did was of no great account but then it occupied him. The doing nothing is not at all a good thing for old people, whereas any little work, no matter how light, keeps up their interest in life, holds them bound up with the present, and preserves them from sudden bodily and mental decay.

The poor old man felt quite strange in our tiny little new place, and he was much touched, too, by the absence of most of the old furniture. I could not let him go back alone, so I went with him.

It happened, unfortunately, whilst I was away, and before my wife had returned, that Ernst came to pay us a visit. Of course, he found the door locked, but he told a neighbour's boy, an old playfellow of his, that an invincible longing for home had made him employ an hour's freedom in rushing off to see his parents. He can't somehow at all get used to his institution. The everlasting reading, writing, and learning by heart—in short, the whole business of study is not at all in his way. His wish is to be put to some trade, and only to learn whatever has reference to that. And I have no doubt whatever of his making a good craftsman. But our Minister of Instruction is of the same opinion that Bebel was of, that all persons are born with about the same amount of intelligence, and that, therefore, they must all alike, up to their eighteenth year (when technical education begins), have the same identical training, as a necessary preparation for the social equality of their after lives.

CHAPTER XIX.

RECREATIONS OF THE PEOPLE.

OPEN-AIR concerts are continually being given in the various public squares of Berlin. The new Chancellor is going the right way to work to make himself popular. In all the theatres there are two performances on week-days, and three on Sundays, and these are all gratis. As a matter of course, the theatres which our busy, industrious Community inherited from the bourgeoisie have proved very inadequate in point of number and size. It has hence been found necessary to supplement them by the addition of various other large buildings. Amongst others, many of the churches are now appropriated to this purpose. As regards the latter, there are still to be found persons here and there who show some scruples, and who somehow do not seem to be able to cut themselves loose from old and deep-rooted superstitions. But it is perfectly clear that the churches have become common property; and it is equally clear, from the provisions of the law framed at the Erfurt Conference of October, 1891, and subsequently adopted, that no common property can be devoted to ecclesiastical or religious purposes.

Naturally, no other plays are given at the theatres than such as represent the glories of the new order, and which keep the sordidness of past capitalists and plunderers in lively remembrance. For any considerable length of time there is, it must be confessed, an element of monotony in this. But, anyhow, it shows up the rightness of our principles, and this is sometimes very necessary.

At first, everyone was at liberty to go to any theatre, just wherever and however he liked. But this senseless competition is now superceded by a well-devised organisation of the people's diversions. It was found that the representations of classic, socialistic plays were made to rows of empty seats, whereas in places where special artistes were engaged, the spectators were packed like sardines. They used to fight almost for the best places. Now all that is different, and the Town Council distributes in rotation to the various theatrical managers the pieces to be represented. The several managers dispose of the seats by lottery to such spectators as have been apportioned to them for that particular evening and play, thus following the plan introduced in 1889 at the socialistic Popular Free Theatre.

There is a saying, "Good luck in love, bad luck at play." And we have experienced the truth of this. As luck would have it, my wife and I have lately, on three successive occasions, got such bad places assigned to us through this lottery system that she could hear nothing, and I found it just as impossible to see anything. She is a little hard of hearing, and I am very short-sighted. Neither of these qualities is in perfect harmony with the idea of social equality as illustrated by the theatre.

Dancing is another of the diversions which are arranged every evening by the city authorities. The entrance is on the same principle as in the case of the theatres, and young and old are all equally entitled to appear. The reform of the etiquette of dancing seemed, at first, to present some few difficulties from a socialistic point of view. This reform has, however, been carried out, and the equality of the ladies is now thereby asserted that the choice of partners made by the ladies alternates regularly with the choice made by the gentlemen. Bebel says, indeed, that women have just the same right to seek that men have to seek them. But the attempt to apply this principle to dancing, by leaving it optional to each sex, in every single dance, to solicit partners, had soon to be abandoned, as it was found that the order of the dances was in danger of becoming involved in inextricable entanglement.

Various interesting letters have appeared in the *Onward*, which discuss, in a very exhaustive and subtle manner, the question whether, in a socialised community, in the dance, such a thing is conceivable as a "right" on the part of certain women to men; or *vice versâ*, a right on the part of men to women? The equal obligation all round to labour, as one lady points out in the *Onward*, clearly entitles all alike to enjoy the same recompense. One part of this recompense is found in joining in those dances which have been organised by the State. No lady could find any pleasure in the dance without a partner of the other sex, whilst it is even more apparent that no gentleman would dance without a lady.

On the part of this lady, the practical solution of the difficulty was suggested in the *Onward*, that for the future all partners at dancing, irrespective of age, beauty, ugliness, and everything else, be chosen by drawing lots. She contends that precisely as in a socialised community there are no persons without work, and without shelter, so in the same way there must never be any ladies at a dance without their proper partners.

But a professor of Modern Natural Law has sent a letter to the paper expressing the fear that, in process of time, this method of organising the selection of partners in the dance might have unforeseen results of an unpleasant kind. He fears it might in time lead to a demand for the recognition of a right of marriage, to a demand that the State take the regulation of marriage into its own hands, by a gigantic universal raffle of men and women. He is strongly of opinion that, precisely as a marriage-tie is a strictly private contract, made without the intervention of any functionary whatever, so in the same way must a temporary union between a lady and a gentleman in the dance preserve the character of a private contract; and he deprecates the idea of any master of the ceremonies meddling, either by lottery or in any other way, with such engagements.

As a matter of fact though, I understand that a large number of ladies take the view that a consistent social equality demands the abolition of the differences between married and unmarried. These ladies have lately joined the party of the Younkers, although in reality they themselves are for the most part of a somewhat ripe age. Anyhow, the extension of the right of voting to women may materially tend to add strength to the Opposition at the approaching election.

Preparations are now being made for a speedy general election. The vast number of calls which the preliminary arrangements for the new socialistic State made upon the time and attention of the Government did not admit of the elections taking place at an earlier date. The right to vote is possessed by all persons of both sexes who have passed their twentieth year. The system of election decided upon is the so-called system of proportional election, which was adopted by the Erfurt Conference in October, 1891. According to this system, large electoral divisions, with several candidates, are constituted, and each political party returns to Parliament a number of representatives in proportion to the votes recorded for that particular party.

CHAPTER XX.

DISAGREEABLE EXPERIENCES.

My wife and Agnes sit up until far into the night, busy with their dressmaking in secret. The work in hand is a new dress for Agnes.

As checker, I ought by rights to denounce the pair of them to the proper authorities for over-production, and for exceeding the maximum hours of labour. Fortunately, however, they are not amongst the fifty persons forming the section which it is my business to control.

The two are even more talkative than usual when engaged in this work of dressmaking. As far as I can make out, they have not been able to find what they

THE SOCIALISTIC FUTURE. 69

wanted at any of the magazines, and so they are altering and adapting some other garments to their fancy. They vie with each other in girding at the new State magazines. Show-windows, puffing, and advertising, sending out lists of prices; all this sort of thing, it seems, has entirely ceased. There is an end to all talk, they complain, of what novelties are to be had, and also to all gossip about prices. The salesmen appointed by the State are all as short in their manner as the officials on State railways always have been. All competition between shops has naturally ceased, and for any certain given article you have to go to one certain magazine, and to no other. This is a necessity of the organisation of production and consumption.

It is, of course, a matter of the most perfect indifference to the salesman whether you buy anything or not. Some of these salesmen scowl as soon as the shop-door is opened, and they have to rise from some thrilling book, or they get interrupted in some other pleasant occupation. The greater the variety of goods you wish to look at, the more questions you ask as to their make and durability, the greater does the ire of the salesman become. Rather than fetch any article from another part of the magazine, he tells you at once they have not got it in stock.

If you wish to purchase ready-made clothing (in this connection I may remark that all private dressmaking and the like, at home, outside of the maximum eight hours day, is prohibited), the outlook is generally a very poor one. The trying-on reminds you of the dressing-up of recruits in barracks, the tailor being profuse in his assurances that the number which corresponds to your measurement must of necessity fit you well. If any garment which has been made to order turns out to be tight here, or baggy there, it needs all the eloquence you are master of to convince the tailor that the garment really is so. If you do not succeed in convincing him, you have either to take the article as it is and make the best of it, or to fight the State in an action at law.

Going to law is now a very cheap affair. As resolved at the Conference of Erfurt in October, 1891, all law is now gratis. As a necessary result of this, the number of judges and lawyers has had to be increased tenfold. But even this large addition is far from sufficing for the requirements, as the actions brought against the State for the inferiority of the goods it supplies, for the wretched condition of the dwellings, the bad quality of the food, the abruptness and rudeness of its salesmen and other officials are as the sand upon the sea-shore.

With the limitations caused by the prescribed eight hours, the courts find it utterly impossible to get through the cases set down in the calendar. Not that lawyers and barristers can be reproached with any wish to unduly prolong suits. So far from this being the case, there are complaints that since the abolition of all fees, and since their appointment as State officials, lawyers scarcely listen at all to what their clients have to say. There would appear to be too great a tendency to settle all differences summarily and in batches. Hence, many persons who do not find an agreeable excitement in the mere fact of going to law, prefer, even in spite of the law's gratuitousness, to put up with any injustice rather than subject themselves to all the running about, loss of time, and vexation of bringing an action.

It is very sad to have to notice that dishonesty is

on the increase, even though gold and silver have quite disappeared. My office as checker lets me into many a secret behind the scenes which I was formerly quite ignorant of. The number of embezzlements is now seven times greater than it used to be. Officials of all grades dispose of goods belonging to the State in consideration of some private favour or service rendered to them personally ; or else they neglect, in the due performance of their duties as salesmen, to extract a coupon of the right value from the money-certificates of buyers, in exchange for goods supplied. In order to make good any deficiency which a lack of coupons would betray, recourse is then had to shortness of weight and measurement, adulteration of goods, and so on.

Thefts of money-certificates are also of frequent occurrence. The photographs with which these are all provided have, in practice, not proved a sufficient safeguard against the use of the certificates by other persons. The promises and presents of all kinds made to persons in high positions, who have nice and easy work to give out, or who otherwise possess influence, constitute an evil which extends to the very highest spheres. We never hold a conference with our head checker without our attention being called to some fresh dodge or trick in reference to these matters.

Hitherto I had always consoled myself with the sure belief that things would get better as soon as we had survived the period of transition ; but now I can scarcely conceal from myself the fact that they get rapidly worse. One of my colleagues tried to explain the cause of this to-day. His explanation is, that since people find the utter impossibility of improving, by honest endeavour and in a legitimate way, that position of equality which has been prescribed for all persons alike, their whole effort is now directed to get, in a dishonest way, that which is in no other way attainable.

CHAPTER XXI.

FLIGHT.

WE have just passed through terrible days. On Sunday morning Franz arrived here unexpectedly on his way to Stettin, to which town, as I take it, he has been transferred. My wife appeared not the least surprised at his coming, but she showed all the more emotion at his going away again. She sobbed aloud, hung upon his neck, and seemed utterly incapable of bearing the separation from her son. Franz parted from me, too, as though it were a matter of never seeing each other more. Agnes was not about at the time, but I heard that they intended to meet at the railway station.

On Wednesday I chanced to read to my wife some intelligence in the *Onward*, that once more a number of emigrants, in seeking to evade pursuit by the frontier guards, had been shot down by the latter. She became greatly excited at the news, and upon my saying, in response to her inquiry, that this had taken place in the roadstead of Sassnitz, she fainted. It took me some considerable time to bring her back to consciousness. Presently she narrated to me in broken sentences that Franz and Agnes had gone off together on Sunday, not, as I had supposed, to Stettin, but to Sassnitz, with the intention of leaving Germany altogether. From the account in the paper, it seems that, upon the arrival of the Danish mail-steamer from Stettin, the frontier guards at once boarded the vessel, and attempted to drag the fugitive emigrants back by sheer force. The emigrants offered resistance, and there was a sanguinary encounter.

They were anxious hours we spent before our fears were somewhat set at rest by the appearance of a new number of the *Onward*, with a list of the killed and arrested. Franz and Agnes were not in either of the lists, but what can have become of them?

My wife now related to me the story of the young people's resolve to get away from the country. It seems that Franz had some time previously confided to her his fixed determination to leave Germany as soon as possible, as he found the state of affairs unbearable. Fearing that my well-known respect for the law might lead me to oppose his intentions, he earnestly begged his mother not to breathe a syllable of his plans to me. All her efforts to induce him to give up the idea were futile. Seeing his determination was unalterable, the good mother could no longer find it in her heart to oppose it. In old days, and quite unknown to me, my wife had laid by sundry gold pieces, and these she gave to Franz to make use of as passage-money on a foreign ship.

At first, Agnes had opposed the plan. She was ready, she said, to follow Franz to the end of the world if needs be; but she could not see at present, she added, what necessity there was for their leaving all else that was dear to them. But in a short time her own circumstances became so unpleasant that she altered her opinion. All this I have only just learnt.

In old days, in the stillness and purity of the maternal home, the young maiden used to carry on her business as a milliner, selling her wares for the most part to a house in a large way. Now she saw herself obliged to work in a big sewing establishment, and to spend the whole day with a number of women and girls, many of whom had habits and principles not at all to her mind. Her chaste maidenliness was often shocked at a good deal of the talk, and at the familiarities between the girls and the male managers. Sundry complaints she made only tended to make her position still more unpleasant. Her personal attractions likewise soon drew upon her an amount of offensive attention from one of the head managers. An abrupt repulse on the part of Agnes only subjected her to those petty annoyances and harassments in her work by which a mean nature seeks its revenge.

I make no manner of doubt that there was plenty of this sort of thing under the old system. But at least there was then this advantage, that people could make a change if anything did not suit them. Nowadays, however, many of the managers seem to look upon their workgirls as little better than defenceless slaves, who are delivered over to them. Many of the higher placed officials see all this well enough, but as they themselves act not a whit differently as regards the abuse of power, they are very lenient in respect of all complaints made to them. Under such circumstances the near relations, or lovers of maidens whose honour is thus menaced, have often no other resource left than to take the law into their own hands. The result of this state of things is, that cases of personal chastisement, manslaughter, and even murder are frightfully on the increase.

Agnes, who only has her mother left, had no protector in Berlin. Her complaining letters to Franz in Leipsig drove him to desperation, and ripened his resolve to no longer delay the execution of his plans. Agnes coincided heartily with his views, and latterly she and my wife sat up half the night to get all ready for the journey.

At length the decisive Sunday had been reached, that Sunday which had given rise to so much anxiety and painful uncertainty to us. The suspense was terrible, but, at last, at the expiration of nearly a week, the arrival of a letter from the English coast put an end to our fears.

According to this letter the pair were fortunately not on board the Danish mail-steamer. The fisherman at Sassnitz, to whose house they had gone on their arrival there, is a distant relation of my wife's. The letter went on to say that the inhabitants of the coast about there are greatly incensed against the new order of things, because by it they have been largely deprived of the comfortable living they made out of visitors to the different bathing-places. Permission to go to watering-places and health resorts is now only accorded to such persons as are duly recommended by a properly constituted medical commission.

Our wary fisherman strongly opposed all idea of taking a passage by one of the mail-steamers, because a vigilant look-out had latterly been kept on these. Watching his opportunity, and availing himself of the attention of the authorities being engrossed by the affair of the Danish steamer, he put Franz and Agnes on board his fishing smack, and made for the open sea. He took them up as far as Stubbenkammer Point, where he fell in with an English goods steamer returning from Stettin, whose captain readily transferred the fugitives to his vessel. The English, whose trade has been very seriously affected by the new order of things, never lose an opportunity of having a slap at our socialistic Government by giving all the aid they can to persons desirous of leaving the country.

So in a short time Franz and Agnes duly reached England, and now they are already on their way to New York.

Poor children! what a deal they must have gone through! And my good wife, above all; my wife who kept all her cares and troubles so long locked up in her bosom, quite unknown to me! How shall I ever be able to recompense her for all the immense sacrifices she has made as a mother?

CHAPTER XXII.

ANOTHER NEW CHANCELLOR.

The discontent in the country has now reached its culmination upon its becoming generally known that all concerts, and theatres, and other amusements in Berlin are free. The inhabitants of every little insignificant bit of a place demand that the national purse provide them with the same diversions that we have here; and they base their claim upon the acknowledged social equality of all, and upon the right of all to enjoy the same identical recompense for the same labours. They say that even under the best of circumstances they are still placed at a great disadvantage, as every village can't have gas or electric lighting, heating by hot-air pipes, and the like.

THE SOCIALISTIC FUTURE. 77

The *Onward* attempted to soothe the feelings of the people in the country by graceful and appropriate references to the advantages of country life, idyllic remarks upon the enjoyment of nature, and the sweet freshness of the air. This was looked upon as irony, and they wanted to know what enjoyment of Nature there was during heavy rains, or in the long winter evenings?

"What fresh air do we get in the cramped little cottages in the country, or in the stables and shippons?"

Thus they grumbled in letters to the paper.

It was pointed out to them that it had never been any different. They admitted the truth of this, but then went on to say that formerly everyone who did not care to stay in the country was at liberty to remove into a town. Now, however, it was very different, and the countryman was tied to his clod of earth until it pleased the authorities to dispose otherwise of him. And under these circumstances they must look to the State to provide them with just the same amusements as the large towns had. They merely asked for equal rights for all, and no more.

The Chancellor did not at all know what to do. The wise government of a people has unquestionably more knotty points about it than the cleaning of boots and the brushing of clothes. This scheme of planning recreations for the people has been about the only thing he has carried through. But with the best will in the world he could not possibly have a band of music, a circus, and a company of specialists at every street-crossing. Pondering upon this business, the happy thought occurred to him to have a few hundred thousand Berliners transferred to the enjoyments of the country every Sunday, and a corresponding number of country people brought up to the attractions of the town. But unfortunately for this social equality the weather proved very unequal. In rainy weather the Berlin people showed no great liking for damp excursions into the country. But the country people, who had arrived in great numbers, naturally expected those seats at the various places of amusement which the Berliners did not care to relinquish.

After the Chancellor had succeeded in thus setting the townspeople and the country people thoroughly at loggerheads with each other, his retirement was deemed expedient, in order that the feeling against him might not unduly prejudice the coming general elections. In Berlin, as might be expected, the disgust at the stoppage of all further free recreations is universal. Henceforth places at the theatres and similar entertainments can only be had against payment in the coupons of the money-certificates.

The Secretary to the Treasury has been appointed as the Chancellor's successor. He is known as a man who goes straight to the point, regardless of all considerations, and he also has the reputation of being a good financier. This latter quality will be all the more welcome, as there are all sorts of ugly whispers abroad respecting the disproportion there is between income and expenditure in the finances of the socialised Community.

CHAPTER XXIII.

FOREIGN COMPLICATIONS.

THE entire navy left by the late Government is to be got ready for service with all possible speed. In addition to this, the standing army, which had already been increased to 500,000 men with a view the better to maintain order at home, and to keep a good watch on the frontiers, has been still further strengthened. These are amongst the first measures taken by the new Chancellor to avert dangers which menace us from abroad.

In the speech which the Foreign Secretary made before the Committee of Government, and in which he unfolded the above measures, he calls attention to the necessity there is for them, in consequence of the deplorable growth of friction, of complications and dissensions with foreign powers. But it must distinctly be understood that the Minister for Foreign Affairs was in no way responsible for this unfortunate state of things. In the socialised Community it was the province of this Minister to arrange with foreign powers for the barter of all goods between State and State. It resulted from this arrangement that all complaints in respect of inferiority of goods, or unpunctuality in supplying them, had to be attended to in the form of diplomatic notes. All that tension which sometimes ensued from the breaking off of business connections, from the jealousies of competition, or from similar commercial causes, and which formerly had only affected mercantile circles, was now transferred to the direct relations which one nation had with another. This is in the nature of the new arrangements.

The Minister went on to say it had been hoped that the almost universal consciousness of having adopted right principles, and the sentiment of the brotherhood of all nations, would play a different part than had been found to be the case in actual practice, toning down differences, and bringing universal peace. He said it need occasion no surprise that the English, that egotistical Manchester race, and their American cousins, would have nothing at all to do with Socialism. They never could get over it that the socialistic European continent, by the repudiation of all State bonds, shares, and so on, had shaken off all slavish indebtedness to English holders of continental scrip. But even these inveterate lovers of money ought to see that Germany had lost unnumbered millions more by the repudiation than it had gained. This was evident, inasmuch as all the Russian, Austrian, Italian and other bonds in German hands had also been repudiated by the socialistic governments of those countries.

These various socialistic governments do not thank us a bit for having, in our lofty consciousness of the international value of Socialism, accepted without a murmur the abolition of all claims for interest on such foreign bonds as were in our possession. Several of these governments have latterly become so egotistical, and they show such a want of regard for us, that they positively go the length of refusing to let us have any goods except against either money down, or an equivalent value in such other goods as they may require. Payment in money was no difficulty to our Government so long as any of those stocks of coined and uncoined gold and silver which had become worthless to us were left. But now that we have by degrees got to the end of our stock of noble metals, we are constantly coming across all kinds of obstacles in the way of the exchange of our goods for commodities which we need from other countries, such as corn, timber, flax, cotton, wool, petroleum, coffee, etc. These obstructions are not confined to the snobbish gentlemen of England and America, but they are every bit as numerous on the part of the neighbouring socialistic nations. Our requirements for the articles just mentioned have not diminished one atom under our socialistic form of government. Quite the reverse. But the neighbouring States, with similar views to our own, tell us that since the introduction of the socialistic form of government they find no demand at all for German goods, such as velvets, shawls, ribbons, mantles, embroideries, gloves, pianos, glass and similar wares. They say that since the restoration of the precise balance of social equality, they produce more of these goods themselves than there is a demand for.

The English and Americans, in their enmity to Socialism, are everlastingly drumming it into us that our manufactures, from ironware and textile goods down to stockings and toys, have so deteriorated under the new system of manufacture, that they can no longer pay us the old prices; and they say that unless an improvement takes place they will have to look to other sources of supply. But even as it is, with the enhanced cost of production, we cannot make our trade pay. All attempts to settle an international maximum working-day have failed, as the various socialistic governments allow particular interests to influence them, and pretend that in this matter they must be guided by such special features as climate, national character, and the like.

What is our Government to do in this dilemma? The fact that we, on our part, now require no more silk, and no more expensive wines from abroad, is but a meagre compensation for the loss of our export trade, amounting to many millions. It can occasion no surprise that the exchange of diplomatic notes partakes daily of an increasingly irritable character. Already, both on the West and on the East, hints have fallen that the right thing for Germany to do, seeing she seems incapable of maintaining her population, would be for her to cede slices of the country to neighbouring States. Nay, the question is even debated whether it would not be advisable, as a precautionary measure, to lay an attachment on these border lands, as security for the bill which Germany had run up for goods supplied to her.

Foreign holders of German bonds who feel themselves injured by our repudiation, take every opportunity of indemnifying themselves by laying an embargo on German vessels and merchandise. Then again, the assistance given by foreign ships to fugitives from our country, is a permanent cause of angry representations.

In short, the hope that the advent of Socialism everywhere would prove synonymous with the reign of eternal peace between the nations, was so far from being realised that the very opposite threatened. The Minister concluded his speech by saying that the Committee of Government could hence hardly fail to see the necessity there was for the navy being again fitted out for service; and it would doubtless also sanction the increase of the army to a million men.

CHAPTER XXIV.

THE ELECTION STIR.

THE general election is at last to take place, and next Sunday is fixed as the polling day. This choice of a day of rest and leisure deserves the highest commendation, as nowadays a hundred times more issues depend upon the result of an election than was formerly the case. Laws are everything in a socialistic State; the law has to prescribe to each separate individual how long he must labour, how much he has to eat and drink, how he must be dressed, housed and what not.

This is already very apparent in the addresses to constituents, and in the election cries. The number of parties which advocate particular interests is legion. Many of the addresses issued by the candidates bristle with proposals for the reform of the daily bills of fare, for the increase of the meat rations, for better beer, stronger coffee, (since the complications with various foreign powers, we scarcely ever get any coffee that is not made exclusively of chicory,) for finer houses, better heating apparatus, more splendid lighting, cheaper clothes, whiter underlinen, etc. etc.

Many women are extremely indignant at the rejection of their demand that one half of the representatives in the various divisions be of their sex. The ground for this rejection was that the demand was a reactionary endeavour to split up the interests of the whole Community into separate interests. The women, however, on their part, fear that, by throwing in their lot with the men, and having divisions common to both, many of their voters will in the end go over to the men's side. They fear that the result of this, coupled with the other fact that the support of women candidates by men is not at all to be relied on, will be that they will be able to carry but a limited number of candidates.

A large number of women, quite irrespective of age, have now thrown in their lot with the Younkers, and this party, the better to render the new alliance permanent, has inscribed upon its banner the right of all women to marriage. These politicians are now constantly appealing to Bebel's book on woman, and they want to make out that they are the real genuine Bebelites. Their programme is—A four hours' maximum working-day; four weeks' holiday in the year for everybody, with a sojourn at the sea-side or in the country; the re-introduction of free amusements; weekly change in the kind of labour to be performed; and lastly, the monthly duration of all appointments to high offices and offices of State (including the office of Chancellor), all such appointments to be held in rotation by all persons in the State, without distinction. The Government party shows considerable confidence, although, in reality, the programme it has issued does not go beyond ordinary commonplace; but it calls upon all other parties, as true patriots, to forget their differences, and to unite and form a grand Party of Order, in opposition to the party of negation and demolition, which was stealthily increasing, and which, under the enticing name of a Party of Freedom, sought to ingratiate itself with the nation. This so-called party of freedom demands the re-recognition of the right of parents to bring up their children, abolition of the State cookshops, free choice of trades and professions, entire liberty to move about as one pleases, and a better recompense for the higher kinds of labour. Now, it is abundantly clear that the concession of demands such as these must of necessity upset all equality, and be eminently calculated to sap the very foundations of Socialism. The candidates of the Government party very properly point out in their addresses to constituents that the granting of such demands would inevitably open the door to the return of personal possessions, the doctrine of inheritance, the sovereignty of wealth, and the plundering system of bygone days.

But, after all, the amount of excitement shown at the present election is strangely out of proportion to the number and many-sidedness of the election cries. In old days people took a good deal more interest in an election. People can now say what they think. Following the resolutions passed at the Erfurt Conference, in October, 1891, all such laws as tended to limit freedom of speech and the right of combination are now abrogated ; but what is the good of a free press so long as the Government is in possession of every printing establishment ? What is the right of public meeting worth when every single meeting-hall belongs to the Government ? True, the public halls, when not already engaged, may be taken by parties of all shades of politics for purposes of public meeting. Only, as it chances, it is just the various Opposition parties that invariably have such ill-luck in this way. As often as they want a hall or a room, they find it has been previously engaged, so they are unable to hold a meeting. The press organs of the Government are in duty bound to insert such election notices from all parties as are paid for as advertisements ; but by an unfortunate oversight at the issue of the money-certificates, there were no coupons supplied for such particular purposes. The unpleasant result of this omission is a total lack of all funds with which to pay the expenses of an election. In this respect the Socialists were vastly better off under the old style. They then had large sums at their disposal, and it must be admitted they knew how to apply them judiciously.

The Opposition parties complain bitterly of the scarcity of persons who, when it comes to the test, have the requisite courage to boldly face the Government as opponents, either as candidates for Parliament or as speakers at election meetings. The fact that every obnoxious person may be unceremoniously told off by the Government to some other occupation, or sent away to a distant part of the country, may have something to do with this hanging back. Such sudden changes involve frequently the endurance of many unpleasantnesses and hardships, particularly to people of riper years. Of course everybody has the right to protest against a transfer which looks like mere caprice on the part of the Government. But how can an individual undertake to prove that the transfer was not a well-advised step, and not justified by other alterations elsewhere in the general labour scheme, which rendered this particular appointment necessary?

The daily conferences which we controllers have together, make it more and more clear that the minds of men, both in the towns and in the country, are in a bad ferment. It is impossible to resist the conviction that the most trifling cause might, at any moment, suffice to call forth a violent eruption of popular feeling in favour of a restoration of the old order of things. From all parts of the country reports are constantly coming in, detailing violent collisions between civilians and the troops which were sent out to establish Socialism. The Government is not even quite sure of the troops. This is the reason why Berlin, in spite of the great augmentation of the army, has not received any garrison. But our police force, on the other hand, which has been picked from the ranks of perfectly reliable Socialists throughout the whole country, has been increased to 30,000 men. In addition to mounted police, the police force is now further strengthened by the addition of artillery and pioneers.

The voting takes place by means of voting-papers, which bear the official stamp, and which are handed in in sealed envelopes. But in view of the system of espionage in the hands of the Government, which penetrates into everyone's most private affairs; in view of the publicity which everybody's life now has, and the system of control that all are subject to; in view of these things, many persons seem to mistrust the apparent security and secrecy of the voting-papers, and not to vote according to their inmost convictions. In former times, somewhat of this sort of thing prevailed in small electoral districts. Now, however, every single individual is a spy on his neighbour.

There is, hence, a great deal of uncertainty as to the result of the elections. If the nation gives expression to its real wishes, we shall see the return of a majority bent upon a restoration of the old order of things. But if these wishes are kept in check by fear, we shall get a parliament which is a mere tool in the hands of the Government.

I do not yet at all know, for my part, how I shall vote. I fancy, somehow, that through my son's flight a sharp eye is being kept on me. I shall most likely end by giving in a blank voting-paper.

CHAPTER XXV.

SAD NEWS.

ANNIE, our dear, precious, little Annie, is dead! It seems impossible to actually realise that the pretty, little creature that used to frolic about, so full of life and joy, is now all at once cold and lifeless; that those young lips which prattled away so sweetly are now for ever dumb; that those laughing eyes that used to shine so brightly are now closed in the stillness of death.

And to-day, too, is her birthday. My wife had gone in the morning to the Children's Home in the hope of, at least, being able to see the child for a few minutes. With a smile on her face, and her heart brimful of joy, she inquired for Annie. A pause ensued, and then she was asked again for her name and address. Presently the news was broken to her that the child had died during the night, of quinsy, and that a message to this effect was now on its way to the parents.

My wife sank down on a chair perfectly stupefied. But the mother's love for her child soon brought her strength back again. She refused to credit such a thing, to believe that her Annie, her child, could be dead; there must be a strange mistake somewhere. She hastily followed the attendant to the death-room. Ah! there had been no mistake. There lay Annie, our dear little Annie, in that still long sleep from which no calling, and no kissing, and no bitter agony of the poor mother will ever awaken her.

What avails it to enter into a long account of the

suddenness with which this malignant disease had attacked her? It began with a cold which she had probably caught at night. At home the child always had a way of kicking off the bed-clothes in her sleep. But yonder there is no mother's eye to watch tenderly at the bedside of each little one amongst so many hundreds. Then again, the prescribed ventilation always causes more or less draught in the bedrooms. Or possibly the child had not been properly dried after a bath. In all these great establishments a good part of the work must unavoidably be done in a summary manner. It is likely enough, too, that the different style of living had made the child a little weaker, and therefore more susceptible than she had been at home. But what avails now inquiry or speculation? All that will never bring our Annie back to life again.

How will my poor wife be able to stand all this sorrow upon sorrow? The shock had such a serious effect upon her that she had to be taken in a cab straight from the Children's Home to the hospital. Later on they fetched me. Annie had been the pet of the family, the only girl, born some time after the lads. How many had been our hopes, our dreams, for her welfare, when she should be once grown up?

I must break the news to-morrow to Ernst as best I can. It will not do for grandfather to get to hear it at all. He can never more tell her stories as she sits on his lap, as she so often used to, and ask again and again to be told about "Little Red Riding Hood and the Wolf."

Franz and Agnes in America have as yet no suspicion of our sorrow, and they won't get my letter before nine or ten days. Franz loved his little sister tenderly, and it was rarely that he omitted to bring her some trifle when coming home from work. The little rogue knew this well enough, and used to run to meet him on the stairs as soon as there was any sign of his coming.

And now there is an end to all these things; an end to these and to so many other things in a few short months.

CHAPTER XXVI.

THE RESULT OF THE ELECTIONS.

WITH heaviness such as this in the heart, all political matters seem so immaterial and idle to one. The sorrows of the present moment make one regard all considerations for the future with indifference.

Franz has proved to be right in his forecast of the results of the elections. In his last letter he expressed his belief that, in a community in which there was no longer any personal or commercial freedom, even the freest form of government would fail to restore any political independence. He considered that those subjects who are so dependent upon the Government, even in the most ordinary affairs of life, as is now the case with us, would only in very rare instances have the courage to vote, no matter how secret that voting might be, in opposition to the known wishes of those in power. The right of voting, Franz wrote, could have no more serious significance in our socialistic State of society than such a right has for soldiers in barracks, or for prisoners in gaol.

The result of the elections shows that the Government party, in spite of all the wide-spread discontent there is, has secured two-thirds of the votes recorded. And this triumph, moreover, has been obtained without any special efforts on their part. The only exception which must be made in this connection was the transfer of a few leaders of the party of freedom, and of the Younkers, which transfers were obviously made for political reasons, and intended to act as warnings.

Weighed down by the load of adversity which has befallen us as a family, I relinquished my original intention of giving an adverse vote, and sided with the Government. Whatever would have become of my wife and me if, in our present frame of mind, I had been sent away to some far-off little place in the provinces?

It seems somewhat odd that in the country, where the discontent is at its height, the Government has scored the best results. The only explanation is, that as people in the country are even more under surveillance than is the case in thickly-populated towns, they are still more reticent in giving expression to opposition views than townspeople are. In addition to this, the recent increase of the army has sent some terror into men's hearts in the disaffected districts.

In Berlin, the Government party is in a minority. And as, according to the system of proportional election now adopted, Berlin forms only one electoral division, the vote of our city is on the side of the Party of Freedom.

The Younkers have come off very badly, and, in spite of the strong support given them by the Woman's Universal Wedlock League, have only succeeded in returning one candidate. It seems pretty clear that the nation has no desire to see any additions made to the socialistic edifice now erected. And even this one candidate would scarcely have been returned but for the help of friends belonging to the Party of Freedom, who supported his election because of the vigorous attacks he made on the Government.

The Party of Freedom, or the Friends of Freedom, as they also style themselves, have obtained nearly one-third of the total number of votes recorded throughout the whole country. And this result has been obtained in spite of all the efforts made by the Government side to brand them as a party of demolition, and one that sought only to undermine the established order of society.

The relative measure of success which this party has obtained is largely owing to the support given by women voters, and, indeed, these latter have shown a good deal more activity in the elections than the voters of the rougher sex. They have made no secret of the bitterness they feel at the present state of things, and of their chagrin at the restrictions placed upon private and domestic affairs.

In particular, the regulation rendering it possible at any moment to give notice of the dissolution of marriage, had the effect of making a large number of deserted wives specially active in the distribution of voting-papers, and in bringing dilatory voters up to the poll.

Of lady candidates only one has been returned to Parliament, this one being the wife of the new Chancellor. This lady is not an adherent of the Government party, but calls herself an entirely independent member. In her election speeches she has repeatedly assured her hearers that she would, in

Parliament, follow exactly the same course she had always adopted at home, both towards her present husband, and towards the husbands she has had before, and plainly speak out her mind whenever the welfare of the nation seemed to require it. The Government party did not care to oppose the election of this lady, partly out of courtesy to the Chancellor, and partly in order that her return might serve as an illustration of the equality of women's rights with those of men.

CHAPTER XXVII.

A LARGE DEFICIT.

A DEFICIT of a milliard per month! A thousand million marks expenditure over income per month! That was the disagreeable message with which the Chancellor greeted the assembling of the new Parliament. The only wonder is that this could be kept secret until after the elections. But it is now high time to look into this matter, and see that some improvement is made.

For a long time past there have been signs in all directions that something or other was wrong. When going to make purchases you were told, only too often, that such and such an article had just run out of stock, and that a fresh supply would not come in for some little time. It now comes out, however, that this was due, not to an increase in the demand, but to a decrease in the supply. Things got so bad that there was often the greatest difficulty experienced in obtaining the most indispensable articles of clothing.

In the case of other articles of daily use you had frequently either to go without, or to put up with the most old-fashioned and antiquated things which had been left on hand ever so long. All import goods, such as coffee, petroleum, farinaceous foods, and so on, were so high in price as to be scarcely procurable.

Indeed, in no respects can it be said that the people have lived in luxury and riot. At dinner, the meat rations have remained nominally the same as at first, *viz.* one-third of a pound per head. But, latterly, there have been unpleasant innovations in respect of including bone, gristle, fat and similar unprofitable matter in the gross weight of the rations. The vegetable part of the bill of fare has been also much simplified, and is now restricted to potatoes, peas, beans, and lentils. On Bebel day the increased meat ration and the free glass of beer which had been looked for were conspicuous by their absence. The strictest economy extends even to the matter of pepper, salt, and spices. On all hands there are complaints that the tastelessness and sameness of the dishes are such as to produce nausea, even in those who have the most robust appetites. What little conversation there is at meal times tends more and more in the direction of talk about sickness and internal complaints.

So far as appearances seem to indicate, our population, in spite of the considerable emigration which has taken place, may count upon a rapid increase as a result of the undertaking on the part of the State to bring up all children free of cost. But notwithstanding this, no measures are taken to meet the demand, and even here in Berlin there is scarcely any building going on. Even the most indispensable repairs are constantly being postponed. No longer is there a syllable dropped about alterations and improvements anywhere; about the renewal of machinery and stores; about the building of new mills, or works, or the enlargement of old ones; or about the construction of new railways.

All stores for daily consumption seem to have dwindled down to a minimum. The only stocks we have are of such things that there is little or no demand for. What other stocks there are consist of such goods as we formerly sent abroad, but which there is now, especially in socialistic countries, no longer any sale for. These goods are gloves, silks, velvets, pianos, wines, embroidered and fancy goods, etc. etc. All such articles may now be had in the home-markets at less than cost price, for the mere sake of getting rid of them.

From month to month the deficit seems to grow greater instead of less, in spite of all attempts to grapple with the difficulty. Even the stocks of raw material and auxiliary material begin to show signs of not being long able to keep the various works fully going. Foreign merchants everywhere have ceased sending any goods to Germany on credit, or otherwise than against an immediate exchange of goods to the same value.

Unpromising as this state of affairs looks, the Government cannot really be reproached with having regulated consumption without a due amount of previous forethought. From the statement made at the opening of the new Parliament, it seems that, from pretty accurate calculations made, the value of the entire productivity of the country, immediately anterior to the Revolution, had been from 17 to 18 milliards of marks annually. The Government took this as a basis, and did not even calculate on any possible increase in the value of the nation's productivity under a new system of things. It simply went on the assumption that this value would remain at least the same, and would not diminish through the maximum working-day being fixed at eight hours. The calculation of the amount of consumption per head of the population was based upon this assumption. But even if the Government had proved right, it is quite evident that the majority of the nation has so far not been placed on a better footing, but on a worse one, than it was in before the great Revolution, to say nothing of all the restrictions placed upon personal and commercial liberty.

A short time, however, sufficed to show that the value of the nation's productiveness sank down to one-third of what it had formerly been. From 18 milliard marks a year it went down to six milliards, or from one and a half milliards per month to half a milliard. In this way we have a deficit of a milliard per month. In four months this amounts to a loss equal to the war contribution which France had to pay to Germany in the great war of past days.

What will this land us in? and where are we to look for help? The next sitting of Parliament is awaited with considerable excitement and interest, as the Chancellor intends then to go into the reasons of the deficit.

CHAPTER XXVIII.

DOMESTIC AFFAIRS.

I FIND myself still quite solitary at home, a thing I have never known since I was a single young man.

My poor wife still lingers on at the hospital, and the doctor lately asked me to make as few visits as I possibly could to her, so that she might be kept from all excitement. For she no sooner sees me than she throws her arms passionately round my neck, as though I had just been rescued from some alarming danger. When I have to leave her there is a renewal of these agitating scenes, and it is long before she can reconcile herself to the idea of my going. After the conversations we have had together, her thoughts naturally wander back to me and the other members of the family; and the more she suffers them to run in this groove the more anxiety and uncertainty does she feel on our account. She is constantly fancying us exposed to all kinds of dreadful persecutions and perils, and is afraid of never seeing us more. The shock her system sustained through the death of our little daughter, and through the events connected with the flight of Franz and Agnes, still affects her most severely.

My wish was to consult our former doctor on her case. He knows her system thoroughly well, as he has attended her, when occasion required, ever since our marriage. When I called upon him he had just returned from a youthful suicide, whom he had in vain endeavoured to call back to life. He told me he was extremely sorry to say that his eight hours maximum working-day had just expired, and that such being the case, he was unable, although much against his will, and in spite of the friendship between us, to give any more medical advice on that day. He told me that he had already, on two occasions, been denounced by a younger colleague, who was not able to render a sufficient number of coupons to the State Book-keeping Department, to prove that he had been engaged professionally for eight hours each day. This young man had laid an information against him for exceeding the hours of labour, and he had been heavily fined for overproduction.

Commenting upon the case he had just returned from, the old gentleman enlarged upon the frightful increase in the number of suicides in the socialistic Community. I asked him whether this one had been a case of unrequited love. He replied in the negative, but went on to say that such cases did sometimes occur, precisely as formerly, as it would scarcely do to prohibit women by act of Parliament from rejecting proposals which were not agreeable to them. The old gentleman who, in his younger days, had been an army surgeon, attributed the increase in the number of suicides to other causes. He told me he had frequently observed that a considerable number of such suicides as took place in the army arose from the simple fact that many young men, although they felt perfectly content in all other respects, found the unaccustomed restraints of military life utterly unbearable. These young men found life under such circumstances unendurable, even although they knew that in the course of two or three years they would return to their accustomed freedom. Hence, it was no wonder, he continued, that the irksome and life-long restrictions of personal freedom which have resulted from the new organisation of production and consumption, together with the idea of the absolute social equality of all, should have had the effect with many persons, and those by no means of an inferior order, of so far robbing life of all its charms, that at last they had recourse to suicide as the only way of escape from the restraints of a dreary and monotonous existence, which all their efforts were powerless to alter. It is very possible the old gentleman is not altogether in the wrong.

It is cheering to reflect that we have good news from Franz and Agnes in America. This is the only ray of sunshine in my life. They write that they have already left the boarding-house in New York, in which they stayed immediately after their marriage, and have managed to get a humble little home together. Through being an excellent hand at his trade, and through his honourable character, Franz has become foreman in a first-class printing concern. Agnes works for a large millinery establishment, and it seems that the wages in this branch have gone up considerably in America since the competition on the part of Germany has fallen so seriously in arrears. Thus, by economy, they are enabled to buy one thing after another for their cosy home. Franz was terribly upset by the news of his little sister's death, and he much wants me to send Ernst over to him, and promises to provide for his future.

No words could describe how sorry I feel for Ernst at his school. And, in fact, as a general thing, one hears nothing but unfavourable accounts of these schools, more particularly of those which are occupied by young men of from eighteen to twenty-one years of age. These young men all know that upon the completion of their twenty-first year, irrespective of what they have learnt, or whether they have learnt much or little, precisely the same fate awaits them all. They know they will find exactly the same course prescribed for them that is prescribed for all alike, and that no efforts or talents will ever avail to enable them to pass beyond that prescribed course. They know, further, that the fact of their tastes lying in this or that particular direction, affords not the slightest guarantee of their receiving an appointment in accordance with those tastes, or even in any approximate accordance with them. The result is, that almost without exception they run into all sorts of extravagance and excess, so that lately such severe measures had to be taken for keeping them within bounds as could scarcely be surpassed in reformatories.

But in spite of all this, I dare not yet venture to whisper a word to Ernst about flight. Even if I could devise a sure way of getting the young fellow on board a foreign vessel, and supposing I had any means of recouping Franz for the expense of the journey, I should still feel incapable of taking such a decisive step for Ernst's future, without his mother's full acquiescence. And to talk to her of such a thing, in her present frame of mind, might be her death.

CHAPTER XXIX.

A STORMY PARLIAMENTARY SITTING.

I HAVE not been in the House since the debate on the savings bank question. It will be remembered that this was prior to the recent general election, and that the House, or as it was styled, the Committee of Government, was then composed exclusively of those members of the Socialist party who had sat before the Revolution, the seats of all the members of the various other parties having been declared vacant, in consideration of the fact that all such members had been returned through the influence of capital. To-day, however, the newly elected opponents of Socialism sat in their places, occupying the entire left side of the House, and numbering about one-third of the seats.

The only lady member who has been returned, the Chancellor's wife, sat in the middle of the front Opposition bench. She is a fine, dashing woman, with plenty of energy: to my thinking she was perhaps a trifle coquettishly attired for the occasion. She followed her husband's speech with marked attention, at one time nodding approval, and at another shaking her head—she wore ringlets, and had red ribbons in her hair—to denote dissent.

The Government side of the House lay under a very apparent cloud of depression, resulting from the news of the large deficit. The Opposition, on the other hand, was very lively in its sallies. The strangers' galleries were densely packed, the number of women present being especially large, and the excitement everywhere considerable.

A debate on the condition of the national finances was down for the order of the day, and I will endeavour to reproduce here the main points of the debate as to the causes of the great deficit. The first speaker was

The Chancellor—" The fact of a considerable diminution in productive values having taken place in our country, a diminution so great that those values are now only one-third of what they were before the great Revolution, is a fact that it ill becomes us either to be-laugh or to be-weep, but which we must all endeavour to grasp and to comprehend. Prominent amongst the causes of that retrogression are the opponents of our socialistic system."

The Member for Hagen, on the Left—" Oh, oh."

The Chancellor—" I need scarcely remind the Member for Hagen that in order to establish Socialism in the country, we have been under the necessity of increasing the police force more than tenfold. In addition to this, we have seen the expediency of doubling the strength of the navy, and of the standing army, so that these forces might be in a position to render adequate support to the police in their work of maintaining order and preventing emigration, and might also constitute a sufficient bulwark against dangers from abroad. Furthermore, the declaring void all State bonds and values on the part of the various socialistic governments of Europe, has necessarily affected whatever German capital was invested in those countries, and in this way greatly tended to lessen our income. Our export trade has fallen off to an alarming extent, partly owing to the Socialist order of things which now reigns supreme in many countries, and partly to the aversion which the bourgeois nations show to our manufacturing system. In respect of these various causes it can hardly be anticipated that there will be much alteration in the future.

" A fruitful cause, in our view, of the great falling-off in the nation's productive power has been the release of young and old persons from the obligation to labour (hear, hear, from the Left), and the shortening of the hours of labour. (Uproar.) We are also further of opinion that the abolition of all piece-work has, undoubtedly, contributed to a diminution of manufacture. (Hear, hear, from the Left). One result of the demoralising effects of the former state of society is, that, unfortunately, the consciousness of the indispensable necessity that is laid upon all persons alike, in a socialistic community, to labour, has not even yet penetrated the bulk of the people to such an extent (dissent from the Right), that we should feel justified in not laying before you the measure we are about to introduce, *viz.* a bill to extend the maximum working-day to twelve hours. (Sensation.) In addition to this, we propose—at least as a provisional measure, and until such time as a satisfactory balance shall have been restored—to extend the obligation to work to all persons between the ages of fourteen and seventy-five, instead of, as hitherto, to those between the ages of twenty-one and sixty-five. (Hear, hear, from the Left.) We shall, however, in these arrangements, make provision for affording facilities to talented young persons for their further culture, and shall also take care that decrepit persons are engaged in a kind of labour that shall not militate against their state of health.

"In the next place, we are strongly of opinion that a plainer and less expensive system of national nourishment than has hitherto been adopted (dissent from the Right) would very materially aid in reducing the deficit. Carefully conducted investigations which we have recently made have fully established the fact that, providing the rations of potatoes and vegetables be increased in a proportionate degree, the customary one-third of a pound of meat is by no means a requisite ingredient of the chief meal of the day, but that one-tenth of a pound of meat, or fat, is abundantly sufficient."

The Member for Hagen—"In Ploezensee!"[1]

The President—"I must request the Member for Hagen to discontinue these interruptions." (Applause from the Right.)

The Chancellor—"It is a well-known fact that there are many estimable persons—I allude to those persons who are styled vegetarians—who hold not only that meat may very well be dispensed with altogether, but that it is positively injurious to the human system. (Uproar from the Right.)

"One of the main sources, however, from which we calculate upon effecting economy, is the placing of narrower bounds to individual caprice as manifested in the purchase of articles. A measure of this nature is a necessary and logical step in the direction of social equality, and we hope, by its means, to put an end to the irrational rule of supply and demand which even nowadays to a great extent obtains, and which so much tends to place obstacles in the way of production, and to raise the price of things correspondingly. The Community produces, let us say, articles of consumption, furniture, clothes, and so on. But the demand for these articles is regulated by the merest freak or caprice—call it fashion, taste, or whatever you like."

The Chancellor's lady—"Oh, oh."

The Chancellor hesitated a moment, and sought by means of a glass of water to calm his evident irritation at this interruption. He then continued—

"I repeat, the caprice of fashion is directed only too frequently, not to those articles which are already

---

[1] Ploezensee is a house of correction in Berlin.

in stock, but to some new-fangled thing which takes the fancy of the moment. As a result of this, those goods which are manufactured and exposed for sale by the Community become often so-called shop-veterans, or they spoil—in short, fail to fulfil the purpose for which they were produced; and all this, forsooth, just because these goods do not quite take the fancy of Mr. and Mrs. X. Y. Z. Now I put the question to you: are we justified in so far yielding to the caprices of such persons, that we offer them a choice of various goods to one and the same identical end—such as nourishment, furnishing, and attire—in order that Mr. and Mrs. X. may live, and dress, and furnish their house differently from Mr. and Mrs. Y.? Just reflect how vastly all processes of manufacture would be cheapened if, in place of having any variety in goods which are destined to fulfil the same purpose, all such articles were limited to a few patterns, or, better still, if they were all made on one single pattern. All losses arising from goods being left on hand as unsaleable, would be avoided if it were, once for all, definitely understood that Mr. and Mrs. X. Y. Z. had to dine, and attire themselves, and furnish their houses in that manner which had been prescribed by the State.

"Hence, lady and gentlemen, the Government contemplates shortly submitting to your consideration plans for regulating your other meals in a manner similar to that which was adopted from the first for the regulation of the chief meal of the day. It will also tend to promote more real social equality if all household goods and chattels, such as bedding, tables, chairs, wardrobes, linen, etc. etc., be declared the property of the State. By means of each separate dwelling being furnished by the State with these various requisites, all after one identical pattern, and all remaining as a permanent part of each dwelling, the trouble and expense of removal are done away with. And only then, when we shall have advanced thus far, shall we be in a position to approach, at least approximately, the principle of equality as respects the question of dwelling-houses, no matter how different their situations and advantages. This problem we propose to solve by a universal fresh drawing of lots from quarter to quarter. In this way, the chances which everybody has to win a nice suite of apartments on the first-floor front are renewed every quarter of a year. (Laughter from the Left. Applause here and there from the Right.)

"As an additional aid to the promotion of equality, we propose that in future all persons shall attire themselves in garments whose cut, material, and colour, it will be the province of this House to determine beforehand. The length of time during which all garments are to be worn will also be fixed with precision."

The Chancellor's lady—"Never, never."

The dissent shown by this member was taken up by various ladies in the strangers' galleries.

The President—"All marks of approval or disapproval from the strangers' galleries are strictly prohibited."

The Chancellor—"I wish not to be misunderstood. We do not contemplate carrying equality in dress to such a length that all diversities will be entirely abolished. On the contrary, we suggest the wearing of various badges as marks whereby the ladies and gentlemen of the different provinces, towns, and trades, may readily be distinguished from each other at a glance. An arrangement of this kind will materially facilitate the surveillance of individual persons on the part of the checkers appointed by the State for that purpose (hear, hear, from the Left,) and will thus render the present unavoidable increase in the number of those checkers less large than would otherwise have been the case. As you are aware, the number of checkers hitherto has been in the ratio of one to fifty of the population. But with the aid of the arrangement just proposed, the Government is of opinion that the appointment of one checker to every thirty of the population will abundantly suffice to make our country an orderly one in the truest sense of the word, (disturbance and cries of "Tyranny" from the Left; the President touched his gong and requested order,) and to ensure on the part of all a rigorous observance of the laws and regulations respecting the taking of meals, style of dress, manner of living, and so on.

"This is our programme. Should it meet with your approval, we doubt not that a vigorous carrying out of the same will soon have the effect of doing away with the deficit, and of leading the country, on the basis of social equality, to unimagined heights of prosperity and happiness, proportionate to the degree in which, in the course of time, it shakes off and triumphs over the demoralising effects of a former state of society." (Applause from the Right; groans and hisses from the Left.)

The President—" Before proceeding to discuss the measures which have been unfolded by the Chancellor, it would be well for such members as may desire fuller information on any of the points noticed, to avail themselves of the present opportunity to direct short queries to the Chancellor."

The Chancellor said he was prepared to answer at once any questions which might be addressed to him.

A member of the Government party wished the Chancellor to be more explicit respecting the form it was proposed to give to the morning and evening meals; and he further asked whether the measures contemplated would have any retrogressive effect upon the value of the coupons composing the money-certificates.

The Chancellor—"I am thankful to the last speaker for having called my attention to several omissions in my statement. With a view to preventing all overloading of the digestive organs, we propose to reduce the bread rations for adults from one pound and a half per diem to one pound. The large amount of starch which is a constituent part of wheat is particularly liable to fermentation, which, as experience has shown, frequently results in unpleasant internal disorders. In addition to this bread ration, and which, as a matter of course, serves for the whole day, each person will receive one hundred and fifty grains of unroasted coffee, and a quarter of a pint of skimmed milk for breakfast. This will yield one pint of coffee. The Government is fully convinced that a conscientious adherence to these proportions will result in the production of a compound which will be free from those heating and deleterious effects which frequently accompany the use of coffee as a beverage. (Laughter from the Left.)

"The evening meal will be composed of a pint and a half of soup for each adult, care being taken to secure due variety, so that these soups may not pall upon the taste. Rice soup, meal soup, barley soup, bread soup, and potato soup will alternate with each other; and in order to obtain still more variety, half a pint of skimmed milk will occasionally be substituted for the soup ration. On the three chief political holidays of the year—the birthdays of Bebel, Lassalle, and Liebknecht—each adult person will receive half a pound of meat, and a pint of beer for dinner.

"I omitted to mention, too, that once a week there will be an augmentation of each adult person's ration by the addition of a herring. Those persons who prefer to consume their herring at the evening meal are at liberty to do so; and, indeed, this plan has much to commend it, seeing that the mid-day meal is already enriched by one-tenth of a pound of meat.

"Such are the proposals which we submit to Parliament for its sanction. In attempting to formulate the nourishment of the people on simple and natural principles, we have been guided by the consideration that such a system would place us in a position to export all our most valuable products, such as game and poultry, hams, highly esteemed vegetables, the choicer kinds of fish, wine, and so forth. By this means we calculate upon paying the bill for such imports as we require for the sustenance of the people, more particularly corn and coffee.

"As regards the money-certificates, it goes without saying that an extended application of the plan of supplying the people with goods must of necessity have an effect on the value of the coupons corresponding to such application. It is also contemplated in future to supply every dwelling with firing and lighting at a fixed rate, which will be deducted from the money-certificates. Similarly, all washing—naturally up to a certain maximum limit—will be done at the State washing establishments without any direct charge being made.

"Under these circumstances, and seeing that people

will have everything found for them, the Government turned its attention to a consideration of the amount it would be judicious and prudent to fix for each person's private expenses, for what, in fact, is familiarly designated pocket-money, and it appeared to us that for such sundry outlays as would be involved in the purchase of an occasional little extra in the way of eating and drinking, of tobacco, soap, in amusements or occasional trips; in short, in procuring all that the heart could wish, we should not be wrong in going to the extent of a mark per head for every ten days. (Laughter from the Left.) It must be understood that the application of this mark is not to be subject to the slightest limitation, or to any sort of official control. It will thus be apparent that we are far from desiring to unduly restrict individual freedom when moving in legitimate spheres."

A member of the Party of Freedom wished to know the intentions of the Government in regard to the greater dilatoriness and lassitude in the performance of labour, which would presumably ensue upon the lengthening of the working-day to twelve hours. He also asked for an expression of the Government's views on the question of an increase of the population.

The Chancellor—" As regards offences against the obligation to work, the Government recognises the fact that the extension of the hours of labour to twelve hours renders a further elaboration of the system of penalties imperatively necessary; and it proposes to effect this elaboration through a variety of means. Amongst others, I mention the removal of the bed for slighter transgressions; arrest, incarceration in the dark cell, and the lash for repeated offences." (Hisses from the strangers' galleries.)

THE SOCIALISTIC FUTURE.

The President threatened to have the galleries cleared forthwith if his warnings were again disregarded.

The Chancellor—"Let me not be misunderstood as regards the lash. We should not be disposed to recommend the application of more than thirty strokes. The end which the Government seeks by these means to attain is to develop the recognition of the necessity of labour, even in those who constitutionally rebel against the doctrine.

"As respects an increase of the population, we hold firmly to Bebel's principle in the main, that the State must regard the advent of every child as a welcome addition to the cause of Socialism. (Applause from the Right.) But even here it will be necessary to draw the line somewhere, and we can never again allow an unreasonable increase of population to upset the delicately-adjusted equilibrium which will be established by the passage of the proposed measures. Hence, as we shall have an opportunity of more clearly showing when the debate on the budget comes on, we reckon upon largely using the system employed for nourishing the people as an instrument for regulating population. Herein we shall be following a hint we are grateful to Bebel for. Bebel said, with no less beauty than truth, that Socialism is a science which is applied with unwavering purpose and inflexible steadfastness of aim to every sphere of human activity." (Loud applause from the Right.)

The President—"As no member seems desirous of asking any more questions of the Chancellor, we can at once proceed to discuss the matters before the House. I shall follow the plan of nominating alternately speakers from the two great parties, the Right and the Left, and shall begin with the Left. I call upon the Member for Hagen."

The Member for Hagen—"I feel little desire to closely interrogate the Chancellor upon the details of his programme. The fruits of the socialistic order (so-called) of things which we have hitherto seen, and still more those which we may expect from the various measures in prospect, are quite enough to fill the soul with loathing and disgust at the condition of affairs which Socialism has brought about in Germany. (Great uproar from the Right; loud applause from the Left.) Experience shows that the miserable realities even transcend what my departed predecessor predicted would be the condition of things if the socialistic programme were ever actually realised. (Cries from the Right: "Aha, the Falsities man; the Slayer of Socialists.") I notice that the gentlemen of the Right have never been quite able to get over the 'Falsities of Socialism,' by the departed member, Eugene Richter.[1] It is only to be regretted that these gentlemen did not suffer themselves to be converted from their errors, so that they could now with unclouded vision see the connection that all matters of national and international economy have with each other. This annual deficit of twelve milliard marks which we are now face to face with, means the bankruptcy of the social democracy. (Great uproar from the Right.) The Chancellor is entirely on the wrong track when he endeavours to make the opponents of Socialism in any way responsible for the deficit.

"Germany already bristles with soldiers and with police in a way that has never been the case before.

---

[1] "Falsities of Socialism," by Eugene Richter. Berlin, 1890.

But when all the affairs of life, large and small, without exception, shall be subject to the management of the State, you will have to reckon with an additional host of servants appointed to see that the State's bidding be duly carried out. It is, unfortunately, but too true that our export trade is in a wretched plight, but this is attributable solely to the utter turning topsy-turvy of production and consumption which has taken place both here, at home, and in the neighbouring socialistic countries. But even this is far from adequately accounting for a deficit amounting to so many milliards. The Chancellor considers that a part of the blame attaches to the shortening of the hours of labour. But before the Revolution took place, the hours of labour were on an average less than ten hours, and in the course of time this working-day would, in the smooth progress of events, have become gradually shorter in an easy and natural way, and without doing any sudden violence to supply. We must seek the cause of the retrogression in all our manufactures, not so much in a shortening of the working-day as in the inferior quality of our goods now; in short, in the style of loafing about (Oh, oh, from the Right) which has become so general. As in feudal times, labour is now again regarded as a kind of villanage, a slavish toil. The system of giving the same remuneration for labours of the most diverse values; the absence of all prospect of bettering one's condition, no matter how great one's industry and skill; these are elements which are inimical to real love of work for its own sake.

"Another reason why manufacture is no longer productive is, that with the cessation of all private enterprise there has been a disappearance of those careful circumspect leaders in the field of labour who took care that a judicious use was made of all materials, and who more or less regulated supply according to demand. Your managers of to-day lack all real and deep interest in their work; they lack the stimulus which, in bygone days, even the heads of Government establishments received from the competition of private firms. This vast deficit teaches us plainly enough that the man of private enterprise was no plunderer, and no superfluous drone, and that even painstaking labour, when not conducted in an intelligent manner, may turn out to be but a mere waste of force and of material. Then again, your system of working everywhere on a big scale, even in cases to which this system does not in the least adapt itself, operates to retard production.

"What have we come to? In endeavouring to get rid of the disadvantages of the socialistic method of manufacture, you place such restrictions on the freedom of the person, and of commerce, that you turn Germany into one gigantic prison. (Great uproar from the Right; applause from the Left and from the galleries. The President threatened to have the galleries cleared at once if there were any more manifestations of feeling.) The compelling of all alike to work; the equality of the working hours for all; the forcing of persons to certain kinds of labour utterly regardless of their wishes and tastes; these are things which we had hitherto had no experience of outside the walls of penitentiaries. And even in those institutions, the more industrious and skilful inmates had the opportunity given them of earning a trifle in the way of something extra. The similarity to prison life is further maintained through the system of each person's having to occupy a certain dwelling, just as prisoners have their cells apportioned to them. The fixtures which are to form an inseparable portion of each dwelling still further enhance the resemblance to gaol life. Families are torn asunder. And if it were not for the fear of Socialism dying out, you would altogether separate husband and wife, as is done in the lock-up.

"And as it is in respect of labour so is it in regard to rest; and every member of this socialistic Community is tied down to the same prescribed nourishment. I was justified in calling out 'Ploezensee,' as the Chancellor enlightened us as to his bill of fare. I will almost venture to say that the food dispensed in former times to the inmates of the prison was better than that which it is now proposed to feed the nation on. In order that nothing may be wanting to complete the resemblance to a gaol, we have now the same uniform clothes proposed. Overseers are already provided in the persons of the numerous checkers; sentinels, too, are posted to see that those who are condemned to Socialism shall not escape across the frontiers. In our prisons the working-day was a ten hours one, not a twelve hours one. Punishment by the lash, which you have to introduce as an aid in establishing the twelve hours working-day, was no longer resorted to in many prisons, because it was felt it could be dispensed with. To those in gaol there was, at least, the possibility of an act of pardon, which might some day open a path to liberty, even to those who had been condemned to life-long imprisonment. But those who are handed over to your socialistic prison are sentenced for life without hope of escape; the only escape thence is suicide. (Sensation.)

"Your explanation of all this is, that we are at present in a state of transition. Nothing of the sort. Things will get worse and worse the longer the present system lasts. Hitherto you have only descended the topmost steps of those which lead to the abyss. The light of day still reaches you on those upper steps, but you turn away from it. Whatever culture is now extant, whatever schooling, and practice, and skill, are all due to former systems of society. But in our socialistic schools of to-day, both elementary, advanced, and technical, our young people make no progress at all, not from any lack of time, or means of instruction, but merely because no one feels that he is absolutely bound to acquire certain things as stepping stones to future success in life.

"You live upon the capital of culture and of wealth which descended to you as the result of former arrangements of society. So far are you, however, from putting by anything, and from providing for improvements and additions, that you cannot even properly maintain such possessions as we have, but suffer them to fall into decay. There are now no means to keep all these things intact, because in destroying the hope of profit, which induced capitalists to engage in enterprises, you simultaneously prevented all further formation of capital, which in its turn would again have led to new undertakings.

"All higher development of the faculties, no less than all material progress, is at a stand-still since the abolition of free competition. Self-interest used to sharpen the wits of individuals, and bring out their inventiveness. But the emulation of the many who strove in the same field of labour, constantly operated to make common property of the achievements of individuals.

"All the proposals of the Chancellor will prove as powerless in making good the vast deficit, as our attempted organisation, some years ago, of production and consumption in our prisons proved powerless to cover even a third part of the current expenses of those places. In a very short time, in spite of the Chancellor's programme, you will find yourselves face to face with a new and a greater deficit. Hence I counsel you not to be too greatly elated at the advent of children as being welcome additions to Socialism. On the contrary, consider rather how you may best promote a diminution of population. For it is quite certain that, even with the beggarly style of nourishment which the Chancellor is compelled to place in prospect for us, Germany, on the basis of the present order of things, will be able permanently to support but a very thin and sparse population. The same applies, of course, to the neighbouring Socialist countries. The inexorable law of self-preservation will hence compel the Socialists on this side, and on that side, to engage in a deadly struggle, which will last until that superfluity of population, which can only be supported by such forms and systems as you have uprooted, shall have succumbed.

"So far as I am aware, the hope that Bebel once expressed is not yet any nearer its accomplishment—the hope, namely, that in the course of time the desert of Sahara would, by means of irrigation, be turned into fruitful districts, and prove a favourable colonising ground to which to draft off the surplus

Socialist population of Europe. I take it, too, that there is as yet no great liking on the part of those of your side in politics who are superfluous here, to follow the other proposition which Bebel was once good enough to suggest as an outlet for surplus population. That suggestion was the settling in the north of Norway, and in Siberia. (Laughter from the Left.)

"Whether or not it is possible to make a halt in the path of progress to destruction, which we have entered upon, I should scarcely care to venture to say. Many milliards in value have already been destroyed by the Revolution, and it would again require the sacrifice of milliards to restore something like order to the present disorganised condition of affairs.

"Whilst we in old Europe, thanks to your efforts, are fast hastening to ruin and destruction, there arises on the other side of the ocean, ever mightier and wealthier, a power that is settled on the firm basis of personal property and free competition, and whose citizens have never seriously entertained the falsities of Socialism.

"Every day that we delay the extrication of our country from the wretched maze into which an aberration of mind has led it, takes us nearer and nearer to the abyss. Hence I say, 'Down with the socialistic gaol regime! Long live Liberty.'" (Loud applause from the Left and from the galleries. Hissing and uproar from the Right.)

The President called the last speaker to order for the concluding remarks contained in his speech, and gave instructions to clear the galleries immediately, by reason of the repeated manifestations of opinion by the occupants.

The clearance of the galleries occasioned no small amount of trouble. As I had to go with the others, I, unfortunately, can say no more as to the further progress of the sitting. But as the Government has a slavish majority at its back, there can hardly be any doubt as to the passing of the various measures proposed by the Chancellor. Not even the indignation of the Chancellor's lady at the proposed Regulation of Dress Bill will have any effect in altering it.

CHAPTER XXX.

THREATENED STRIKE.

THE Chancellor's new proposals for getting rid of the great deficit have been received on all sides in Berlin with mockery and derision. To what lengths this dissatisfaction may yet go there is no foretelling. For a long time past there has been a great spirit of discontent amongst the artificers in metals, and more particularly amongst engineers. These men claim to have had a large share in bringing about the Revolution, and they complain that they are now shamefully cheated out of what Socialism had always promised them. It certainly cannot be denied that before the great Revolution they had over and over again been promised the *full reward of their labours*. This, as they maintain, had expressly and repeatedly appeared in black and white in the columns of the *Onward*. And shall they now put up with it, that they only receive the same wages as all the others?

They say that if they were to receive the full value

of the machines and tools which are turned out of their shops, after deducting the cost of raw material and auxiliary material, they would get, at least, four times as much as they do now.

It is in vain that the *Onward* has endeavoured to point out to them that their interpretation is an entirely false one. Socialism, says this organ, never contemplated giving to each labourer in his special field the full reward of his work in that particular sphere of labour. It promised the nation as a whole the full reward of the labours effected by the whole people. Whatever these mechanics might turn out of their shops and mills, it was quite clear that the things turned out were not the result purely and simply of hand labour. Expensive machines and tools were equally necessary to their production. In a no less degree were large buildings and considerable means indispensable. All these accessories had not been produced by the workmen actually engaged at the time being. Seeing then that the Community finds all these buildings, plans, and means, it was assuredly only just that the Community should appropriate whatever remained after paying a certain wage calculated at one uniform rate for all persons in the country.

But these mechanics, somehow, cannot be brought to view the thing in this light. They say that if the State, or the Community, or whatever you like to call it, is now to take those profits which formerly were paid to shareholders for the loan of their capital, it comes to much the same thing to them in the long run. If this was to be the end of the affair, the great Revolution might just as well never have taken place at all.

The prospect of the lengthening of the working-day to twelve hours has made these workmen in the different metal trades more bitter than ever. Twelve hours a day at a roaring fire, and at work on hard metals, is a different thing from twelve hours behind a counter waiting for customers, or twelve hours looking after children.

In short, these men demand the full reward of their labour as they understand the term, the working-day being limited to ten hours at the very outside. Several large meetings of the men have already taken place at night on Jungfern Common and Wuhl Common, to debate upon the question of a resort to force should their demands not be conceded. There is talk of the threatened strike embracing 40,000 men, who are engaged in Berlin in the different metal branches.

CHAPTER XXXI.

MENACING DIPLOMATIC NOTES.

THE socialistic Governments of Russia and France are quite as much at their wits' ends as we are to know how to overcome the difficulties that are constantly arising. Hence they try to appease the ill-humours of their populations by directing attention to foreign affairs. One of the first acts of the socialistic governments had been to dissolve the Triple Alliance. Austria sees herself threatened at the present moment by Italy, in Istria and the Italian Tyrol. The opportunity of Austria's being thus engaged on another side appears a favourable one to Russia and France for their adopting a high tone towards Germany. Accordingly, both powers have addressed simultaneous notes to our Foreign Office, requesting that within ten days, payment be made of the amount due for goods supplied.

Now, how is it that France comes to be in the position of a creditor of ours? As a matter of fact, we have drawn nothing whatever from France except a few million bottles of champagne which were emptied in the first intoxication of delight at the success of the great Revolution, and before the State had taken the regulation of consumption into its own hands. Russia, however, has had the perfidy to cede a part of her claims on us to France, in order to construct a common basis of operations against us. Our indebtedness to Russia has now run up to over a milliard, although our imports of corn, wood, flax, hemp, etc., from that country have only been the same as they were in former times. These are imports which we absolutely cannot do without. But the unfortunate part of the business is, that those manufactures which we had been in the habit of sending to France and Russia, in the way of exchange for imports, have of late nearly all been returned to us, on the pretence of their not being at all up to the mark, of the price being too high, and so forth. If such a thing had happened to us in former times, we should simply have paid the Russians in Russian bonds or their coupons, of which there was then no scarcity in Germany. But having now no bonds, and no stock of noble metals to fall back upon, we are rather bothered by the lack of a convenient means of exchange.

Our good neighbours are only too well aware of

this. Hence they take no great pains in their diplomatic notes to conceal the threat, that in case the claims are not promptly settled, they will be compelled to take possession of parts of Posen and Eastern Prussia, and of Alsace and Lorraine as pledges. Both powers expressed their readiness to waive their claims for payment, provided Germany were disposed to yield up possession of these provinces. Is not that a piece of unparalleled impudence?

There is no lack of well-drilled men, of muskets, powder, and shot in Germany. The former regime took good care to provide an abundance of these materials. But in other respects we are not so well prepared; and it seems that in consequence of the diminution in the out-put of coal, and of the dwindling away of the stocks, there is a scarcity of this material which would most seriously hamper the transport of troops by rail. Great complaints are also made by the military authorities as to the scarcity of meat, flour, oats, and similar stores.

Meantime, France has annexed Luxemburg. At the dissolution of the Custom's Union, this Duchy had been, so to say, cut quite adrift. One party in the Duchy took advantage of the ill-humour at the severance of the old commercial relations with Germany to call in the French. The latter lost no time in responding to the call, and they soon reached the territory by way of Longwy. It is said that French cavalry has already been seen on the Germano-Luxemburg frontier close to Treves.

CHAPTER XXXII.

GREAT STRIKE AND SIMULTANEOUS OUTBREAK OF WAR.

ALL the iron-workers in Berlin and the neighbourhood came out on strike this morning, upon the refusal of their demands to receive the full reward of their labour. The Government met the strike with a prompt order to at once stop the dinners and suppers of all those on strike. In all the State cookshops the officials have the strictest instructions not to honour the coupons of the iron-workers. The same suspension of the coupons applies to all restaurants, and all shops whence, in accordance with the Government regulations, these persons in ordinary times derive their supplies. The various shops and places in question are closely watched by strong detachments of police. By these means it is hoped that those on strike will, in a very short time, be starved into submission, inasmuch as the few crumbs and parings which their wives and friends will be able to give them from their rations will be of very little avail.

There is more bad news to follow. An order has just been issued to reduce the bread rations of the entire population by one half, and to do away with the meat rations altogether. It is hoped by these measures to effect such a saving as will enable the Government to, at least to some extent, provision the frontier fortresses. For, in the meantime, the threatened distraints in Germany have actually begun to take place. From the Grand Duchy of Luxemburg, French cavalry has advanced across the German frontier, passed the

Moselle, and interrupted the traffic on the Treves and Diedenhofen, and Treves and Saarlouis lines. Other divisions of the French army, with Longyon, Conflans, Pont-à-Mousson, Nancy, and Lunéville as their bases of action, have crossed the Lorraine frontier with the intention of besieging Metz and Diedenhofen, and making a demonstration in the direction of Morchingen. Both of these fortresses are stated to have but one week's provisions at the outside. The same may be said of Koenigsberg, Thorn, and Graudenz, against which points Russian columns are now on the march, with a view to seizing territory as security for their claims. The tactics appear to be, to attack Eastern Prussia on the East, and on the South at the same moment, so that upon its subjugation the eastern line of attack upon Germany may be much shortened on the one hand, whilst on the other hand the supplies of horses for the German army from Eastern Prussia will be cut off. As far as possible, the reserves hasten to the frontier. But it has unfortunately transpired that there is a great lack of even necessary articles of clothing for many of the reserves. In consequence of the great falling off in manufacture in many branches, after the Revolution, large quantities of underclothing, boots, and other articles intended for the army, had to be diverted to the civilians, seeing that the regular supply did not keep pace with the demand.

But enough of this. I find I shall henceforth be no longer able to give the same full account of events as they happen. The twelve hours day comes into force to-morrow, so I shall then not have much time for writing. I propose, therefore, to finish off this narrative as soon as possible, and to send it to Franz and Agnes in the New World. May it long remind them, and their children, and children's children, of me and of the present stormy times, and, indeed, I must get it off with all possible speed, or it may be too late. I notice that I am regarded with such increasing suspicion that a search might be made, and my papers confiscated at any moment.

CHAPTER XXXIII.

THE COUNTER-REVOLUTION BEGINS.

THE iron-workers on strike have no intention of being starved out. Paying a visit to my father-in-law, I discovered on the way home that a number of these men were about attempting to storm the bread magazine. Grandfather is located at the Refuge for Elderly People, into which Bellevue Castle has been turned. The bread magazine is just opposite Bellevue Castle, on the other side of the Spree, and between the river and the railway embankment. Finding all the entrances well secured, the men on strike set about climbing over the high wall which surrounds the magazine. But as soon as any of them reached the top of the wall, they were picked off by the sentinels stationed inside, and had thus to pay for their temerity with their lives.

The men next took to the railway embankment, which commands a view of the grounds round the magazine. They commenced tearing up the rails, and cutting the telegraph wires, but the musketry-fire from the magazine in a short time killed and wounded so many that the besieging force was soon dislodged from this position.

Their next move was to make for the houses in Luneburg Street, behind the embankment. Having established themselves in the top storeys of those houses, a rattling fire soon began from the top windows on the one hand, and from the magazine on the other. But it soon became clear that the besieged, though small in point of number, were possessed both of better weapons and more ammunition.

Presently fresh detachments of the rioters attempted from Heligoland quay to make a breach in the walls surrounding the magazine. In the meantime, however, and quite unperceived, police reinforcements had been promptly brought up through the grounds of Bellevue Castle. These reinforcements took possession of the foot-bridge, which is almost concealed by the railway-bridge, and from this position opened a murderous fire upon the mass of mostly unarmed persons on Heligoland quay. Uttering wild cries of vengeance, and leaving great numbers of killed and wounded behind them, the mob dispersed in all directions. It is said that artillery has been sent for to cannonade Luneburg Street from the other side of the Spree.

Leaving this scene of carnage, I entered the Zoological Gardens with the intention of making for the south-west side of the city by a circuitous route. The streets in all directions were full of people in the wildest state of excitement. No outrages have so far been committed in the south-west portion of Berlin, but from what they say here it seems that the iron-workers have been more successful in their attacks on the bread stores in Temple Yard and in Kopenick

Street than was the case with the Bellevue magazine. They say, too, that numerous rifles and stores of ammunition have fallen into their hands. It is very difficult to get hold of any really reliable news, but from all accounts the riot on the right side of the Spree seems to be getting rapidly general.

The police force has of late been fixed at 30,000 men. None but fanatical Socialists may serve, and these are chosen from all parts of the country. The force is also supported by strong detachments of artillery and cavalry. But they are dispersed all over the city, and what can they, after all, effect if the two million inhabitants really rise in a general revolt? The smokeless powder of nowadays greatly facilitates the taking of a true aim from an ambuscade, whilst the modern form of rifle is singularly calculated to prove serviceable to those indoors when used under cover of the houses.

Detachments of police, some on foot and some mounted, are continually hurrying with all possible speed towards the centre of the city. From all appearance the whole of the armed force available is being drawn together in the neighbourhood of the palace and unter den Linden. What will be the end of it all?

And poor old grandfather? I found him very dull and apathetic. In the entire absence of a family circle and of surroundings to call forth his interest, his faculties show a very marked decay. He told me the same things several times over, and repeatedly put the same questions to me which I had just before answered. He even mixed up the persons and generations of his own family. A cheerless old age indeed!

CHAPTER XXXIV.

DISHEARTENING NEWS.

To-day has been the saddest day of all my life. On going to see my wife I found that she talked incoherently and wildly, and did not recognise me. The doctor said he must convey the sad intelligence to me that the death of her child and the severe shocks of the last few months had so deeply affected her mind as to leave now no prospect of recovery. She fancies herself constantly exposed to the persecutions of all kinds of demons. It has been held advisable to send her to the Asylum for Incurables, and she is to be taken there to-day.

For five and twenty long years we have shared all our joys and sorrows with each other, and have lived together in the closest affinity, both of heart and mind. And now to behold the partner of my life, all dazed and bewildered, the dear, kindly eyes not even recognising me, is worse than death's separation.

On all sides the storm of revolt increases in fury. But what are all such things to me now, with my load of grief and sorrow? There has been some fighting in Eastern Prussia, and also in Alsace and Lorraine, and our side has everywhere had the worst of it. Our troops had to contend with many disadvantages. They were badly clothed, and insufficiently nourished; and when, after wearisome forced marches, they came face to face with the enemy, they were unable, in spite of all their bravery, to make a permanent stand.

In Berlin, the riot continues to spread. The entire region on the right bank of the Spree, and many other parts of the city and suburbs are quite in the hands of the rioters. The latter are reinforced by an uninterrupted stream of people from the provinces, and it is also said that portions of the army fraternise with the people.

It is hence evident that the revolution was not long in spreading beyond the limits of the iron-workers and their particular demands. It aims now at the abolition of Socialism. And the more I reflect, the more I feel inclined to anathematise myself for having, for so many years, aided in bringing about such a state of affairs as we have experienced during the last few months. My only motive was the sincere belief that Socialism would cause a better order of things for future generations. I believed so then, but I now see that I did not comprehend the whole question. But how can my boys ever forgive me for having helped to bring about those events which have deprived them of their mother and their sister, and utterly destroyed our happiness as a family?

But now I must speak to Ernst, be the consequences what they may. I feel myself impelled to him, so that I may warn him against going out at all just now. Young lads like he is are only too apt to go forth and to mingle in the sin and excitement of a time like this. I have leisure enough now to visit Ernst even in the day-time. Suspected of no longer being sound in politics, I have been deprived of my place as a checker, and told off as a night-scavenger. I only hope my work there will not turn out to be of a horrible nature.

CHAPTER XXXV.

THE LAST CHAPTER.

To Mr. Franz Schmidt, New York.

"My Dear Franz,—Be a man, and prepare yourself to bear with fortitude the sad news this letter conveys. Our dear father is no longer amongst the living. Like many other innocent victims, he has fallen a sacrifice to the great rising which has raged for the last few days in Berlin.

"Father had left home with the intention of calling upon me, and warning me to on no account mix myself up with the commotion in the streets. Close to our school there had shortly before been a fight between the police and the rioters, and some of the police had taken refuge in our school. All this was of course quite unknown to father. A party of the rioters lay in concealment, and in all probability one of these, on seeing him, took him for a government messenger; anyhow, a shot fired from an upper window struck him, and he expired in the course of a few minutes. You may fancy my horror when they brought him into our house, and I found it was my own father.

"He fell a victim to the solicitude he felt for the welfare of his family. In the hope of seeing a better future for those dear to him, he had allied himself with the Socialists, but recent events had entirely cured him of his errors.

"Respecting the sad state of our dear mother, father wrote you lately himself, and also mentioned about poor old grandfather. In all my wretchedness and loneliness, my thoughts are continually turning to you, Franz, across the ocean, as my only human refuge. By the time I post this letter I shall, I hope, have already crossed the German frontier. Towards Holland they say the frontier is pretty open. When once there, I shall be able to make use of the money you sent me.

"Things here are in a frightful condition. Sanguinary defeats on the fields of battle towards the frontiers, and in the country nothing but anarchy and threatened dissolution. How all these things have come about, and got into such a muddle, you will best gather from the diary which father kept down to the very day before his death, and which I will bring with me.

"With best love to you both,

"Your lonely brother,

"Ernst."

POSTSCRIPT.

"IF it be true that 'good wine needs no bush,' it is true that a good play needs no epilogue. Yet to good wine they do use good bushes; and good plays prove the better for the help of good epilogues. What a case am I in then, that am neither a good epilogue, nor cannot insinuate with you in behalf of a good play."

Amongst the various writers who of recent years have painted, for the world's benefit, pictures of the state of society which they conceive would result from a widely extended Socialism, Bellamy and Morris take prominent rank. Perhaps by the time, in the twentieth century, that Socialism is realised, human nature will have undergone such an extraordinary and phenomenal transformation that the views of above-named sanguine gentlemen will prove to have been justified. Let us hope such will be the case.

Meanwhile the talented and clear-sighted Member of Parliament for Hagen, Eugene Richter, pictures to himself a somewhat different state of things as the result of the establishment of Socialism. And his little book may be read, perhaps not quite without advantage, as a slight contribution to the literature of this subject, as presenting the consummation in a different light, and as an expression of what some will doubtless regard as eccentric and extreme views.

In treating a prosy subject of this kind, the mind

has a natural craving to get away now and then from the dry detail of statistics and political economy, and to escape, if only for occasional moments, into an atmosphere of lightness and laughter. So far as English readers are concerned, it is to be regretted that Richter did not see fit to arrange his matter in a less dry and ponderous way, and to introduce an element of fun and ridicule into his treatment of the subject. The English are firmly persuaded that the Germans quite lack all sense of humour. It need hence occasion no surprise that this nation, with that stolidity conventionally ascribed to it by the English, have, nevertheless, read this little book with avidity in editions of hundreds of thousands.

THE TRANSLATOR.

www.ingramcontent.com/pod-product-compliance
Lightning Source LLC
Chambersburg PA
CBHW020101170426
43199CB00009B/360